D1283948

TECHNIQUES AND MATERIALS
of MUSIC

Enhanced
Seventh
Edition

Techniques and Materials of Music From the Common Practice Period Through the Twentieth Century

Thomas Benjamin
Peabody Conservatory
The Johns Hopkins University

Michael Horvit
Moores School of Music
The University of Houston

Timothy Koozin
Moores School of Music
The University of Houston

Robert Nelson
Moores School of Music
The University of Houston

CENGAGE
Learning·

Australia • Brazil • Japan • Korea • Mexico • Singapore • Spain • United Kingdom • United States

Techniques and Materials of Music: From the Common Practice Period Through the Twentieth Century, Enhanced Seventh Edition
Thomas Benjamin, Michael Horvit, Timothy Koozin, Robert Nelson

Product Director: Monica Eckman

Product Manager: Sharon Poore

Content Developer: Nell Pepper

Content Coordinator: Elizabeth Newell

Product Assistant: Rachael Bailey

Media Developer: Chad Kirchner

Marketing Manager: Jillian Borden

Rights Acquisitions Specialist: Jessica Elias

Manufacturing Planner: Julio Esperas

Art and Design Direction: Carolyn Deacy, MPS Limited

Production Management, and Composition: Naman Mahisauria, MPS Limited

Cover Designer: Lisa Buckley

Cover Image: © hudiemm/Getty Images

For product information and technology assistance, contact us at **Cengage Learning Customer & Sales Support, 1-800-354-9706**

For permission to use material from this text or product, submit all requests online at **www.cengage.com/permissions**
Further permissions questions can be emailed to **permissionrequest@cengage.com**

Library of Congress Control Number: 2013954982

ISBN-13: 978-1-285-44617-2

ISBN-10: 1-285-44617-8

Cengage Learning
200 First Stamford Place, 4th Floor
Stamford, CT 06902
USA

Cengage Learning is a leading provider of customized learning solutions with office locations around the globe, including Singapore, the United Kingdom, Australia, Mexico, Brazil and Japan. Locate your local office at **international.cengage.com/region**

Cengage Learning products are represented in Canada by Nelson Education, Ltd.

For your course and learning solutions, visit **www.cengage.com**

Purchase any of our products at your local college store or at our preferred online store **www.cengagebrain.com**

Instructors: Please visit **login.cengage.com** and log in to access instructor-specific resources.

Printed in China
1 2 3 4 5 6 7 17 16 15 14 13

To our wives, friends, colleagues, and students

Contents

What's New in the Enhanced Seventh Edition

- The new **TMMTheory.com** website provides online study guides, examples from music literature with audio, video tutorials, and short quizzes to reinforce key concepts in the book. An online record tracks the student's progress. The site is compatible with popular Web browsers for computers and mobile tablets.

- The revised and expanded e-Workbook provides exercises in PDF format for all units in the book. A new volume to complement Part 1 offers comprehensive exercises on musical rudiments. New composition exercises in varied textures are integrated in the eWorkbook. Registered users of the book can download the e-Workbook at **TMMTheory.com**.

Getting Started

1. Create your user account for member access to the **TMMTheory.com** website.

   Students: Follow the instructions on the card included with your book to create your online user account. Do not loose the access code printed on the card. Only registered users have full access the website.

   Instructors: To set up an instructor's account, go to login.cengage.com. Once set up, it should take 24 hours to authenticate your account. If you do not receive verification within that time frame, please contact your sales rep by going to http://sites.cengage.com/RepFinder/ to find your direct sales representative and their current email.

2. Explore the online content at **http://TMMTheory.com** as you study in the book. Refer to the Help page at the website for more information.

Preface

Techniques and Materials of Music, Enhanced Seventh Edition, is intended to be used as a text for the first two years of college theory courses, not including ear training and sight-singing. The subject matter includes a study of the rudiments of musical materials; the harmonic, melodic, rhythmic, and basic formal procedures of the common practice period; and an introduction to the compositional techniques developed during the twentieth century. Entering students without strong backgrounds might need to take a preliminary course in rudiments, or, at minimum, spend the first month or so using a separate fundamentals workbook.

This book fills a need that standard theory textbooks do not satisfy. Many texts present their material in an elaborate prose format that locks the teacher into the author's method of presentation down to the smallest details. This allows for very little creativity and flexibility in the classroom. It often results in the unimaginative and educationally unproductive procedure of reading the text in class together with the students, underlining or outlining the text to distill its essentials, or ignoring the text as peripheral to the course. Many theory teachers who know their material well use no text at all because of these drawbacks.

Techniques and Materials of Music is a complete common practice theory text that also covers contemporary materials. It presents its subject matter in concise outline form, enabling the teacher to flesh out the course in a personal manner. It allows for flexibility and creativity on the part of the teacher, which leads to more direct communication and interaction between student and teacher. Students are presented with what they need to know in an accessible format.

This text grew out of our classroom experiences at the University of Houston and the institutions with which we were previously connected.

The result of extensive classroom testing, it originated as a series of mimeographed handouts that were gradually refined and reorganized until they coalesced into their current form. It embodies our belief that directness and leanness of approach are desirable, as well as a firm conviction that the focus of any music course should be *on the music itself.* Toward this end, the book is intended to be used with a well-organized anthology of graduated musical examples, such as our *Music for Analysis, Seventh Edition* (New York: Oxford, 2009), whose content and organization exactly parallel this text. This allows the student to see the larger context in which the material under study occurs and to see it used in a variety of styles and textures.

The material is organized in outline form. In each unit, a general procedure is followed: the material is described as clearly and concisely as possible, and skeletal examples of the procedures under consideration, in both keyboard and choral voicings, are interwoven with the explanatory material. The website provides tutorials and musical examples to reinforce key concepts presented in the book. The teacher and the students are continually urged to refer to *Music for Analysis* or other anthologies for musical examples that employ the techniques under discussion. This is *essential* to the approach of this book.

The text and accompanying e-Workbook contain several types of exercises. There are melodies and figured and unfigured basses for harmonization. Simple two- and three-note basses and simple figured basses have now been added to Units 3 through 8 in Part II. Every effort has been made to ensure that all exercises are as musical as possible and that the cumulative level of these exercises reflects and is relevant to the level of the students' development. Further, there are exercises of a more creative, compositional nature, such as completing exercises in a given texture or composing small forms, and exercises dealing with instrumental textures, both keyboard and chamber combinations (intended to be performed in class by the students).

An essential feature of the book is Part V, which presents summaries of several important topics. Most of this material is developed in a gradual fashion throughout the text as appropriate to each of the units. Here, however, the students can find in one place a summary of such topics as doubling, voice leading, chord-choice criteria, and so forth. Throughout the text, the student is directed to Part V for such topics as textures, motive and sequence, contrapuntal techniques, and analytical procedures, to name only a few.

Part V also contains a complete and concise discussion of form at all levels: phrase and period, small forms such as binary and ternary, contrapuntal forms, variations, and large forms such as sonata-allegro and rondo. Students are referred to the discussion of form at the appropriate point in the presentation of the harmonic materials.

The approach is eclectic rather than idiosyncratic. The terminology is standard: that in general use in the United States today. Where more than one term is commonly in use, the alternate term is also given. Relevance to actual musical practice has been our primary concern. That is why we require the use of an anthology: the student should have in hand a maximum amount of music literature from which to learn.

We wish to thank the following persons, whose comments helped us in planning the Seventh Edition of *Techniques and Materials of Music*: Francis Brancaleone of Manhattanville College; Amy Dunker of Clarke University; Gayle Murchison of College of William and Mary; Sharon Nauman of University of Akron; London Shavers of Northwest Mississippi Community College; Lori Shipley of Hampton University; Patrick Smith of Virginia Commonwealth University; and Robert Templeman.

T.B.
M.H.
T.K.
R.N.

Suggestions to the Instructor

The following comments reflect the way in which we have used this book and are intended only to be general guidelines.

1. Analysis

Many examples from the literature, with as broad a stylistic scope as possible, must be used in presenting the material of each unit; all examples must be played in class. For this reason we recommend the adoption of a supplementary music anthology. Our *Music for Analysis* contains excerpts and complete pieces from the common practice period and the twentieth century and is organized for use with this book. Several other suitable anthologies are listed in the Bibliography.

The instructor should go beyond mere harmonic analysis in discussion. Constant reference should be made in analysis and in criticism of student writing to such important matters as motivic unity, melodic construction, counterpoint, cadence and phrase structure, harmonic rhythm, and any special features of a given work. For a more complete listing of elements, see the Checklist for Analysis, Part V, Unit 21.

Stylistic and historical aspects of the music are in a sense incidental in analysis, but they may be considered to give an extra dimension to the discussion. Problems of performance as they are clarified by analysis often interest students.

In class discussion the instructor should emphasize the organic nature of music—that is, the interactions of line, rhythm, harmony, and so on. It may be pedagogically useful to treat all elements separately at first, but the unifying aspects should be brought out as early as possible. Complete short works should be studied periodically to show large-scale applications of various materials and techniques.

For analysis the instructor should choose music that exhibits a wide variety of textures, instrumental idioms, and harmonic rhythms, as well as avoid overdependence on the four-voice chorale style.

2. Reference materials

Continual use of the reference section (Part V) for summaries and detailed explanations is urged. Most of the topics covered in it are broadly applicable throughout the text. Of particular interest are the units dealing with form (Units 13, 14, and 20)

3. Written work

Statements regarding doubling and voice leading within Parts II and III apply to strict four-part writing. Obviously the musical examples will exhibit a wider variety of procedures as a result of the textures and idioms employed. There are more exercises in each unit than most instructors will find practical to use. These exercises range from basic part-writing work to exercises in various textures and styles. It is hoped that the instructor will make use of a wide spectrum of exercises.

In the creative writing exercises the instructor should make use of the various instruments and voices available in class. He or she should discuss all instruments to be used and refer to the information on instrument ranges found in Part V, Unit 23.

All student writing in which there is any degree of creativity should be played in class and discussed. Musicality, as well as technical competence, should be emphasized.

A complete collection of supplementary exercises can be found in an e-Workbook at the premium web site. This e-Workbook in PDF format provides more than 200 pages of exercises to complement this textbook. Included are preliminary exercises, melodies for harmonization, figured and unfigured basses, and compositional exercises that explore a wide variety of textures and styles. This comprehensive collection of graded exercises covers the full range of tonal harmony and post-tonal techniques introduced in the textbook.

4. Keyboard applications

Keyboard application of all basic material in this text is strongly recommended. Any of the available keyboard harmony textbooks may be used.

5. Sight-singing and ear training

It is assumed that sight-singing is an integral part of the theory program. We suggest doing as much part-singing as possible. Several good collections of music for singing, such as the authors' *Music for Sight-Singing, Fourth Edition* (Belmont: Schirmer/Cengage, 2005), are available.

Both sight-singing and ear-training work should be coordinated with the theory course. Instructors may wish to use *Music for Ear Training, Fourth Edition* (Belmont: Schirmer/Cengage Learning, 2013). This book is also coordinated with *Techniques and Materials of Music*. The instructor should stress the importance of listening to both written and analytical assignments before students hand them in.

6. Improvisation

Three types of exercises in this book lend themselves to classroom improvisation: melodies for harmonization, figured-bass exercises, and phrase-chord formats. These may be done with piano alone, piano plus instruments, or groups of instruments without piano.

7. Rudiments of music

Part I is intended as a review of musical fundamentals. When dealing with a class whose background in rudiments is not strong the instructor may wish to use a fundamentals text. Many of these texts now come with CDs containing computer exercises that allow the students to drill on their own.

8. Analytical symbols

The analytical system used throughout employs roman numerals to indicate chord function and quality, together with traditional figured-bass symbols that show inversion, precise interval structure, and chromatic alterations. The instructor may of course use any modification of this system desired.

TECHNIQUES AND MATERIALS
of MUSIC

PART 1

Rudiments

1 The Great Staff and Piano Keyboard

There are several ways to name pitches in practice today. The lowest C on the piano may be called "CC" in the "Contra" octave. A more scientific system designates the lowest C on the piano as C1, with each octave up from C numbered consecutively. Using this terminology, middle C is C4.

Clefs

treble clef (G clef)   alto clef (C clef)   tenor clef (C clef)   bass clef (F clef)

eWorkbook exercises, online tutorials, and musical examples with audio for this unit are available at the *Techniques and Materials of Music* website, **TMMTheory.com**.

Visit the TMM website

Accidentals

I. An *accidental* is a sign at the left of a musical note that indicates a change in the note's pitch.

A. ♯ A *sharp* raises the pitch of a note one half step above its natural pitch.

 = one half step higher than

B. ✕ A *double sharp* raises the pitch of a note two half steps above its natural pitch.

 = two half steps higher than

C. ♭ A *flat* lowers the pitch of a note one half step below its natural pitch.

 = one half step below

D. ♭♭ A *double flat* lowers the pitch of a note two half steps below its natural pitch.

 = two half steps below

E. ♮ A *natural* cancels an accidental previously in effect.

*This pitch is G natural.

*This pitch is F natural.

II. To restore a double sharped or a double flatted note to its original pitch, a single accidental is sufficient.

*This note is C sharp.

*This note is D flat.

III. Accidentals are often carelessly written, even in some printed music. The following observations on the proper use of accidentals in tonal music should be carefully noted.

    A. Accidentals do not carry into other octaves in the same measure; one should specify the desired accidental.

    B. Though a bar-line technically cancels an accidental from the preceding measure, one should specify the desired accidental in the new measure, in parentheses.

    C. If there is an accidental early in a measure, it is wise to restate it parenthetically later in the same measure.

IV. Pitches that sound the same but are spelled differently are called *enharmonic.*

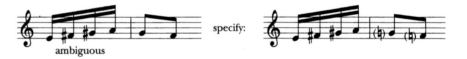

    G♯ = A♭   E♭ = D♯   C✕ = D

eWorkbook exercises, online tutorials, and musical examples with audio for this unit are available at the *Techniques and Materials of Music* website, **TMMTheory.com**.

Visit the
TMM website

3 Intervals

I. An *interval* is the distance between two pitches.

    A. This distance is measured by the number of whole and/or half steps it contains.

    B. The names for intervals correspond to the number of different names of notes the interval contains.

        1. The distance from C to E is a third (contains three note names: C, D, and E).

        2. The distance from C to B is a seventh (contains seven note names: C, D, E, F, G, A, and B).

        3. The size of an interval is indicated by an arabic numeral (for example, third = 3).

    C. Intervals are classified as major (M), minor (m), perfect (P), diminished (d), and augmented (A).

        1. 1, 4, 5, and 8 may be only P, d, or A.

        2. 2, 3, 6, and 7 may be only M, m, d, or A.

II. The following intervals are contained within the span of an octave:

P1, or perfect unison (prime) = 2 notes on same pitch

m2, or minor second = $\frac{1}{2}$ step

M2, or major second = 1 step

m3, or minor third = $1\frac{1}{2}$ steps (M2 + m2)

M3, or major third = 2 steps (M2 + M2)

P4, or perfect fourth = $2\frac{1}{2}$ steps (M3 + m2)

A4, or augmented fourth = 3 steps (M3 + M2)*

d5, or diminished fifth = 3 steps (P4 + m2)*

P5, or perfect fifth = $3\frac{1}{2}$ steps (M3 + m3; or P4 + M2)

m6, or minor sixth = 4 steps (P5 + m2)

M6, or major sixth = $4\frac{1}{2}$ steps (P5 + M2)

m7, or minor seventh = 5 steps (P5 + m3)

M7, or major seventh = $5\frac{1}{2}$ steps (P5 + M3)

P8, or perfect octave = 6 steps (P5 + P4)

*See enharmonic intervals, IV, pg. 7

III. Relationships of interval classifications.

    A. Major intervals are one half step larger than minor intervals.

    B. Augmented intervals are one half step larger than perfect or major intervals.

    C. Diminished intervals are one half step smaller than perfect or minor intervals.

IV. Intervals that sound the same pitches but are spelled differently and thus function differently are called *enharmonic intervals*.

V. The d5 and A4 are enharmonic intervals (see IV-B for an example). Both these intervals contain three whole steps (tones), and both are commonly referred to as the *tritone (T) intervals*.

VI. Intervals that are larger than an octave are referred to as *compound intervals*.

    A. P8 + M2 = M9

    B. P8 + m3 = m10

VII. Inversion of intervals.

    A. An interval is inverted by transferring its lower note into the higher octave or by transferring its higher note into the lower octave.

B. Major intervals invert to minor intervals, and minor intervals invert to major intervals.

   1. m2 inverts to M7, and M7 inverts to m2.

   2. M2 inverts to m7, and m7 inverts to M2.

   3. m3 inverts to M6, and M6 inverts to m3.

   4. M3 inverts to m6, and m6 inverts to M3.

C. Perfect intervals invert to perfect intervals.

D. Augmented intervals invert to diminished intervals, and diminished intervals invert to augmented intervals.

   1. d5 inverts to A4, and A4 inverts to d5.

   2. A6 inverts to d3, and d3 inverts to A6.

   3. d7 inverts to A2, and A2 inverts to d7.

VIII. A *harmonic interval* is one in which the pitches are sounded simultaneously.

IX. A melodic interval is one in which the pitches are sounded consecutively.

X. Note that when the same accidental is applied to both notes of an interval, the size remains the same.

XI. In tonal music, intervals are classified as either *consonant* (stable) or *dissonant* (unstable).*

    A. Consonances

        1. Perfect consonances include P1, P5, P8, and P4 (depending upon the context).

        2. Imperfect consonances include m3, M3, m6, and M6.

    B. Dissonances include m2, M2, m7, M7; all augmented and diminished intervals; and P4 (depending upon the context).

XII. A summary of all the diatonic intervals found within the major and minor scales will be found in the next unit.

📱 *Visit the TMM website*

eWorkbook exercises, online tutorials, and musical examples with audio for this unit are available at the *Techniques and Materials of Music* website, **TMMTheory.com**.

Exercises

1. Identify the following intervals:

a.

b.

---

*Refer to Part V, Unit 2, for a discussion of the overtone series.

2. Write the notes that form the indicated intervals above the given pitch.

a.

b.

c.

d.

e.

3. Write the notes that form the indicated intervals below the given pitch.

a.

b.

c.

d.

e.

4. Invert the given intervals. Identify both the given and inverted intervals:

5. Name the bracketed intervals in the following melodies:

   a.   Symphony No. 4, first movement

Brahms

b.   *Tristan und Isolde*, Act 3   Wagner

4 Major and Minor Scales

I. The following succession of intervals, demonstrated with the C-major scale, is needed to construct a *major scale* above any given tonic (key-note). The following symbols are used to indicate the size of the steps (seconds) between successive notes: ∧ denotes a major second, and ⌒ denotes a minor second.

Following are the other intervals present in the C-major scale.

A. Sevenths.

| M7 | m7 | m7 | M7 | m7 | m7 | m7 |

B. Thirds and sixths.

| m6 | M6 | M6 | m6 | m6 | M6 | M6 |

| M3 | m3 | m3 | M3 | M3 | m3 | m3 |

C. Fourths and fifths.

| P5 | P5 | P5 | d5 | P5 | P5 | P5 |

| P4 | P4 | P4 | A4 | P4 | P4 | P4 |

II. *Minor scales* have three traditional theoretical forms—natural (pure), harmonic, and melodic—shown here with the A-minor scale. There is rarely a clear distinction between these forms in actual music. Context alone determines which forms of the variable sixth and seventh scale-degrees will be used in a given passage. In the following chart, the symbol ⌐¬ is used to indicate the augmented second:

natural (pure)   (same)

In all minor scale-forms, scale-degrees one through five are invariable. The natural and harmonic forms are the same ascending and descending, whereas the melodic form is variable. All alterations are to the sixth and seventh degrees. The descending form of the melodic minor is the same as the natural minor.

Following are the other intervals present in the C-natural minor scale.

A. Sevenths:

B. Thirds and sixths:

C. Fourths and fifths:

III. Scale-degree names:

1 is the tonic.

2 is the supertonic.

3 is the mediant.

4 is the subdominant.

5 is the dominant.

6 is the submediant.

7 is the subtonic (when an M2 below tonic).

7 is the leading tone (when an m2 below tonic).

eWorkbook exercises, online tutorials, and musical examples with audio for this unit are available at the *Techniques and Materials of Music* website, **TMMTheory.com**.

Visit the
TMM website

Exercises

1. Write the following major scales up one octave from tonic to tonic, using the treble staff: G, F, A, E♭, B, D♭. Use accidentals as they are required to form the proper interval series. Do not use key signatures.

2. Write the following major scales according to the instructions for Exercise 1, using the bass staff: D, B♭, E, A♭, F♯, G♭.

3. Write the following major scales according to the instructions for Exercise 1, using the alto clef: G, B♭, A.

4. Write the following major scales, using the tenor clef: F, D, E♭.

5. Write the following minor scales, according to the instructions for Exercise 1, in both treble and bass staves:

Natural	Harmonic	Melodic
e♭	d	e♭
a	b♭	g♯
b	c♯	e

The natural and harmonic forms may be written only ascending; the melodic form must be written both ascending and descending.

6. Write the following minor scales as above, using both alto and tenor clefs: a♭, b, c.

5 Key Signatures

I. *Key signatures* arise from the need for certain consistent accidentals within keys (that is, to secure the desired scale-form above a given tonic). Here is the D-major scale and key signature:

II. Each major key has a *relative minor* whose tonic is on the sixth scale-degree of the major (and a minor third below the tonic) and that uses the same key signature. In harmonic analysis, a major key is indicated by an uppercase letter followed by a colon, and a minor key by a lowercase letter followed by a colon; thus e is the relative of G.

III. Parallel major and minor keys have the same tonic; thus F major is the parallel of F minor. *Parallel keys* have signatures that differ by three accidentals.

F: f:

IV. Charts of key signatures.

A. For the "sharp" keys, successive tonics are related by ascending perfect fifths.

major key:	C	G	D	A	E	B	F♯	C♯
relative:	a	e	b	f♯	c♯	g♯	d♯	a♯

B. For the "flat" keys, successive tonics are related by descending perfect fifths.

major key:	C	F	B♭	E♭	A♭	D♭	G♭	C♭
relative:	a	d	g	c	f	b♭	e♭	a♭

V. The order in which key signatures are written on the staff is given as follows. Sharps are read from left to right and flats from right to left.

$\sharp\!\rightarrow$

F C G D A E B

$\leftarrow\!\flat$

VI. The *circle of fifths* is a traditional graphic arrangement that shows the major and minor keys with their key signatures.

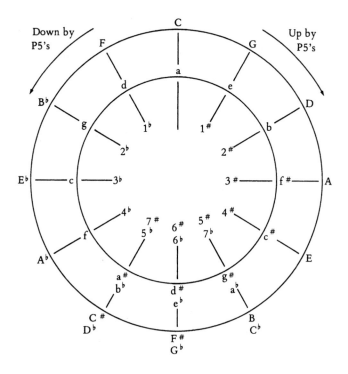

VII. Keys whose tonics are enharmonic are themselves enharmonic. Composers will often use the enharmonic equivalent of a key in situations where the enharmonic key contains fewer accidentals.

Visit the TMM website eWorkbook exercises, online tutorials, and musical examples with audio for this unit are available at the *Techniques and Materials of Music* website, **TMMTheory.com**.

Exercises

1. Using the great staff, write the following key signatures: D, B♭, A, E♭, B, D♭, g, b, c, f, f♯, e.

2. Give the relative and parallel keys for the following keys: C, E, a, d, g♯, c♯, F♯, C♯.

3. Using key signatures and accidentals as needed, write the following minor scales in both staves of the great staff:

Natural	Harmonic	Melodic
b	e	c
c♯	b♭	f♯
f	g♯	g
d	e♭	a♭

Using key signatures and accidentals as needed, write the following minor scales in both the alto and tenor clefs:

Natural	Harmonic	Melodic
g♯	c♯	a♯
b♭	g	d
c	e	e♭
f♯	f	b

6 Triads

I. A *triad* is a three-tone chord consisting of superimposed thirds. The lowest note is called the *root*; the middle note is called the *third*; and the uppermost note is called the *fifth*.

A. A *major triad* has the following intervallic structure: M3 between root and third, m3 between third and fifth, and P5 between root and fifth.

B. A *minor triad* has the following intervallic structure: m3 between root and third, M3 between third and fifth, and P5 between root and fifth.

C. An *augmented triad* has the following intervallic structure: M3 between root and third, M3 between third and fifth, and A5 between root and fifth.

D. A *diminished triad* has the following intervallic structure: m3 between root and third, m3 between third and fifth, and d5 between root and fifth.

eWorkbook exercises, online tutorials, and musical examples with audio for this unit are available at the *Techniques and Materials of Music* website, **TMMTheory.com**.

Visit the
TMM website

Exercises

1. Construct triads of the indicated quality.

a. Root given:

b. Third given:

c. Fifth given:

2. Construct the following triads using three notes only on the treble staff and using accidentals as required: E major, C minor, F♯ diminished, B♭ augmented, C♯ minor, G diminished, A augmented, D♭ major, A major, E♭ minor.

3. Construct the following triads using three notes only on the bass staff and using accidentals as required: B♭ minor, D major, A diminished, F♯ augmented, C diminished, E♭ major, G♯ minor, A♭ augmented, E minor, A♯ diminished.

7 Meter and Rhythm

I. Note value and rests.

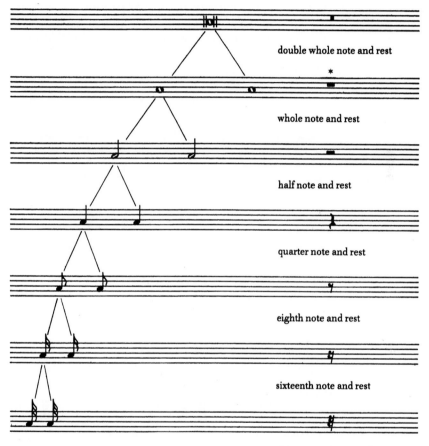

double whole note and rest

whole note and rest

half note and rest

quarter note and rest

eighth note and rest

sixteenth note and rest

thirty-second note and rest

A. Dots add half the value of the note; a second dot adds half the value of the first dot.

*A whole rest is often used to indicate the total duration of a measure regardless of the meter.

B. Other durations may be achieved by use of the tie. The tie must be used for durations extending from one measure to another.

II. *Meter* is the organization of musical time into recurring patterns of accent (stress). Each complete pattern constitutes a *measure,* and the measures are divided by *bar-lines.* The particular pattern is indicated by a *meter signature (time signature).* The first beat of every measure is called the *downbeat.*

Common Metric Patterns

> = accented   ⌣ = unaccented

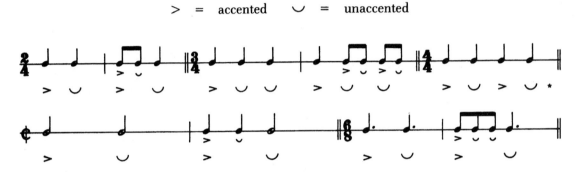

Note that a similar alternation of accent and unaccent is found in the division of the beat.

Meter Signatures

	Simple		Compound	
Duple				
(beat unit) $\frac{2}{2}$ ¢	𝅗𝅥	𝅗𝅥	$\frac{6}{4}$ 𝅗𝅥.	𝅗𝅥.
(background unit)	♩ ♩	♩ ♩	♩ ♩ ♩	♩ ♩ ♩
$\frac{2}{4}$	♩	♩	$\frac{6}{8}$ ♩.	♩.
	♫	♫	♪♪♪	♪♪♪
$\frac{2}{8}$	♪	♪	$\frac{6}{16}$ ♪.	♪.
	♬	♬	♬♬	♬♬

---

*In earlier common practice styles no distinction is made between the first and third beats. However, in later styles the two are differentiated; the first beat becomes a primary accent and the third beat a secondary accent.

	Simple		**Compound**	
Triple	$\frac{3}{2}$	(notation)	$\frac{9}{4}$	(notation)
	$\frac{3}{4}$	(notation)	$\frac{9}{8}$	(notation)
	$\frac{3}{8}$	(notation)	$\frac{9}{16}$	(notation)
Quadruple	$\frac{4}{2}$	(notation)	$\frac{12}{4}$	(notation)
	$\frac{4}{4}$ C	(notation)	$\frac{12}{8}$	(notation)
	$\frac{4}{8}$	(notation)	$\frac{12}{16}$	(notation)

A. Meters are classified according to the number of background units and the number of beats per measure. The *background unit* is the note value representing the largest possible division of the beat unit, as shown in the table above. *Simple meters* have two background units per beat; *compound meters* have three background units per beat. (Note that consequently the beat units of compound meters are always dotted notes.) Meters having two beats per bar are *duple*; three beats per bar, *triple*; four beats per bar, *quadruple*; and five beats per bar, *quintuple**.

In simple meters the upper number of the time signature indicates the number of beats, and the lower number indicates the note value of the beat. In compound meters the upper number indicates the number of background units; and the lower number the value of the background unit. To find the number of beats in compound meter, divide the upper number by 3.

The meter signature is placed after the key signature on the first system and is not repeated on subsequent systems.

---

*Quintuple meter is often termed a *composite meter*, as it can be considered a combination of duple and triple meters. See Part IV, Unit 3.

B. *Related meters* are meters having the same number of beats and the same type of division of the beat (either simple or compound) but different beat values, for example, $\frac{2}{4}$ and $\frac{2}{8}$. (Refer to the table on meter signatures.)

C. *Equivalent meters* are meters having the same number of beats and the same background unit but different divisions of the beat. For example, $\frac{2}{4}$ and $\frac{6}{8}$ both have two beats per measure and a background unit of the eighth note. However, $\frac{2}{4}$ has two eighth notes per beat, whereas $\frac{6}{8}$ has three eighth notes per beat. Divisions in compound meter can be expressed in simple meter by use of the triplet figure; simple into compound, by use of the duplet.

III. *Rhythm* generally refers to the actual choice and distribution of notes within a bar. Beyond the need to have the total value of the notes equal the value indicated by the meter signature, certain notational conventions should be considered. Groups of notes with flags are generally connected by *beams*.

These groupings should reflect the meter.

Beams are preferable to single stems and flags except in vocal music, which traditionally gives each syllable a separate note.

IV. Establishment of meter.

   A. *Agogic accent* is the use of relatively longer note values to establish meter.

   B. *Melodic pitch patterns* establish accent through melodic patterning.

   = triple grouping ($\frac{3}{4}$)

   = duple grouping ($\frac{2}{4}$)

   = quadruple grouping ($\frac{4}{4}$)

   C. *Accompanimental patterns* may establish metric accent by bass note placement and establish weak beats or parts of beats by chord or inner-voice placement.

   etc.

   etc.

   etc.

D. *Metric stress* may be established by accent marks or dynamics.

V. *Syncopation* is the displacement of accent in which accented notes occur on normally unaccented beats or parts of beats. This displacement can be affected by any of the four devices of establishing meter just described.

A. Agogic accent.

B. Melodic pitch patterns.

C. Accompanimental patterns.

D. Artificial accent.

eWorkbook exercises, online tutorials, and musical examples with audio for this unit are available at the *Techniques and Materials of Music* website, **TMMTheory.com**.

Exercises

1. Complete the following:

   a. Identify the following meter signatures by indicating the number of beats, the note value receiving one beat, the division of the beat, and the terminology for the meter:

Meter	Beats	Unit of Beat	Background Unit	Terminology
$\frac{2}{4}$	two	♩	♪	simple duple
$\frac{3}{4}$				
$\frac{6}{8}$				
$\frac{4}{4}$				
C				
$\frac{2}{2}$				
$\frac{6}{4}$				
$\frac{3}{8}$				
¢				

   b. Complete the chart below:

Meter	Beats	Unit of Beat	Background Unit	Terminology
$\frac{2}{4}$				
				compound duple
¢				
			♪	simple _____
	3	𝅗𝅥		simple _____
$\frac{9}{8}$				
	2	♩.		
			♩	compound triple

2. Give the equivalent number of indicated values for the note shown.

Example: ♩ = 2 eighth notes

a. Undotted note values:

𝅝 _____ half notes

𝅝 _____ quarter notes

𝅝 _____ eighth notes

𝅝 _____ sixteenth notes

𝅗𝅥 _____ quarter notes

𝅗𝅥 _____ eighth notes

𝅗𝅥 _____ sixteenth notes

♩ _____ thirty-second notes

♩ _____ eighth notes

♩ _____ sixteenth notes

♩ _____ thirty-second notes

♪ _____ sixteenth notes

♪ _____ thirty-second notes

𝅘𝅥𝅯 _____ thirty-second notes

b. Dotted note values:

𝅝· _____ half notes

𝅝· _____ quarter notes

𝅝· _____ eighth notes

𝅗𝅥· _____ quarter notes

𝅗𝅥· _____ eighth notes

𝅗𝅥· _____ sixteenth notes

♩· _____ eighth notes

♩· _____ sixteenth notes

𝅗𝅥· _____ thirty-second notes

𝅗𝅥· _____ sixty-fourth notes

♪· _____ sixteenth notes

♪· _____ thirty-second notes

♪· _____ sixty-fourth notes

𝅘𝅥𝅯· _____ thirty-second notes

𝅘𝅥𝅯· _____ sixty-fourth notes

𝅘𝅥𝅰· _____ sixty-fourth notes

c. Tied note values:

𝅝 ‿ 𝅗𝅥 _____ half notes

𝅝 ‿ 𝅗𝅥 _____ quarter notes

𝅗𝅥 ‿ ♪ _____ eighth notes

𝅗𝅥· ‿ 𝅘𝅥𝅯 _____ sixteenth notes

♪ ‿ 𝅘𝅥𝅯 _____ thirty-second notes

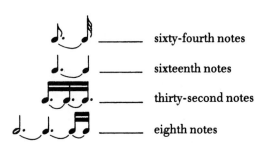

♪· ‿ 𝅘𝅥𝅯 _____ sixty-fourth notes

♩· ‿ ♩ _____ sixteenth notes

𝅘𝅥𝅯· ‿ 𝅘𝅥𝅯· ‿ 𝅘𝅥𝅯 _____ thirty-second notes

𝅗𝅥· ‿ 𝅗𝅥· ‿ ♩ _____ eighth notes

3. The following examples are given ungrouped and without measure bars. Add measure bars, and group eighth notes and smaller values with beams as they would normally appear in the given meter. The first note is always a downbeat.

4. What meter signature does each of the following patterns suggest? Examine the patterns, determine the meter signature of each, add this signature at the beginning of the example, and draw in measure bars. Each example will be *four* full measures.

5. In the following examples replace the ties with dotted notes wherever possible. The duration of each note should remain the same.

6. Notate the following examples in the related meters indicated. In other words, keep the same number of notes in each measure and the same rhythmic relationships, only changing the note values to fit the meter.

Example

Rewrite the following in $\frac{2}{8}$ and $\frac{2}{2}$:

Rewrite the following in $\frac{4}{8}$ and $\frac{4}{2}$:

Rewrite the following in $\frac{6}{16}$ and $\frac{6}{4}$:

7. Rewrite the following examples in the equivalent compound meter:

Example

8. Rewrite the following examples in the equivalent simple meter:

Example

PART 2

Diatonic Materials

Triads in Root Position

I. A triad is in root position if the root is in the bass. A triad takes its name from its root and its intervallic structure. You may wish to review Part I, Unit 6, for a discussion of qualities of triads.

II. Voicing.

   A. In keyboard voicing, soprano, alto, and tenor are on the upper staff; bass is on the lower staff.

   B. In choral voicing, soprano and alto are on the upper staff; tenor and bass are on the lower staff.

III. Directions of stems.

   A. Single voice on the staff: When the note head is on or above the center line (third line) of the staff, the stem goes down; when the note head is below the center line of the staff, the stem goes up.

   B. Two voices on the staff: Stems for the upper voice go up; stems for the lower voice go down.

   C. Three voices on the staff (as in keyboard voicing): When at least two note heads lie above the center line of the staff, the stem goes down; when at least two note heads lie below the center line of the staff, the stem goes up; when the note heads lie equally above and below the center line of the staff, the stem may go in either direction.

IV. Because the triad contains three notes and four voices are to be employed, one tone must be doubled. Initially, only the root is to be doubled. (See the example in II–A and II–B.)

V. Spacing.

    A. In *close spacing*, the three upper voices are as close together as possible.

    B. In *open spacing*, a tone of the same triad can be placed between each adjacent pair of upper voices (alto and tenor, soprano and alto).

    C. Strict four-part exercises.

        1. Avoid intervals larger than an octave between adjacent upper voices. Any interval between bass and tenor is allowed. In the *incorrect* examples that follow, note the gap between alto and tenor in the first and between soprano and alto in the second:

        2. Maintain the normal order of voices. Soprano is the uppermost voice; alto is the second voice from the top, below soprano and above tenor; tenor is the second voice from the bottom, below alto and above bass; and bass is the lowest voice. In the *incorrect* example that follows, note that tenor is above alto:

D. Choral voice ranges.

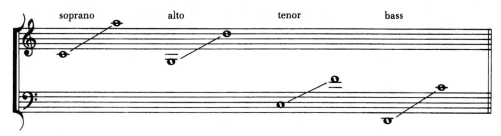

eWorkbook exercises, online tutorials, and musical examples with audio for this unit are available at the *Techniques and Materials of Music* website, **TMMTheory.com**.

Visit the
TMM website

Exercises

In all written work the student should be attentive to the details of musical calligraphy. (Refer to Part V, Unit 1.)

1. Construct the indicated triads in the indicated voicings and spacings, using root position. Check spacing, doubling, and stem directions.

2. Construct the following triads on the great staff in root position in choral close and open spacings and keyboard voicing, using accidentals as required: D major, B♭ major, F major, A minor, A♭ major, B minor, E minor, G major, C minor, and F♯ minor. Use half notes, observing proper stem directions.

The Tonic Triad in Root Position

C: I   c: i

I. The roman numerals I and i refer to the major and minor triads, respectively, built on the first scale-degree *(tonic triad)*. In a major key the tonic triad is major, and in a minor key the tonic triad is minor. The quality of the triad is designated by the roman numeral: uppercase for major and lowercase for minor.

II. Chord function. In common practice music, chords tend to progress in consistent, and thus predictable, patterns. *Function* refers to the tendency of a chord to progress to certain other chords. This system of chord relationships is called *functional tonality*. See also Part V, Unit 8. The tonic triad is used to initiate many progressions and is the ultimate goal for all chord progressions.

III. In strict four-part writing, only the root is to be doubled at this point.

IV. For voice leading in strict four-part writing, refer to Part V, Units 4 and 5, for definitions and a summary of procedures. In chord repetition, wherever possible, keep the same spacing from one chord to the next.

F: I _____   D: I _____   g: i _____

A. In choral voicing a change from close to open spacing or the reverse will often be preferable when an interval larger than a fourth occurs in the soprano. In keyboard voicing, however, the notes in the right hand are always kept in close position. This necessitates overlapping when there is a wide leap in the soprano.

G: I _____   d: i _____   d: i _____

B. Contrary motion can often be achieved through a change of spacing.

Eb: I _____   D: I _____

Students should observe that doubling and voice leading may differ from these norms, depending upon the texture of the musical example being analyzed.

Analysis

Look at the examples in Unit 1 of *Music for Analysis*. Refer to Part V, Units 15 and 17. Consider the following:

1. Characterize the texture. Is it homophonic or contrapuntal? How many voices are there, and does the number change? Also consider range, tessitura, spacing, and instrumental idioms.

2. Is the music motivically organized? If so, identify the motive or motives, and discuss the techniques of motivic development.

3. Given the lack of harmonic progression, do the longer examples still exhibit some sense of form? How is this achieved?

Visit the
TMM website

eWorkbook exercises, online tutorials, and musical examples with audio for this unit are available at the *Techniques and Materials of Music* website, **TMMTheory.com**.

Exercises

1. Harmonize the following soprano lines in the indicated voicings and spacings, using the tonic triad in root position only. Check spacing, doubling, and stem direction, and play each individual voice.

G: I _____   D: I _____   F: I _____

2. Harmonize the following two- and four-note sopranos in both keyboard and choral voicings, using the tonic triad in root position *only*. Close or open choral spacing will be determined by the register of the soprano. Below each example, give the roman numeral analysis of the chord. (*Note:* The given notes should appear as the highest voice [soprano], and the stem directions must be adjusted to suit the type of voicing involved.)

3 Connection of Tonic and Dominant Triads in Root Position

I. The roman numeral V refers to the major triad built on the fifth degree of the scale *(dominant triad)*. In minor keys the third of the dominant triad, the *leading tone*, must be raised. The accidental that affects the leading tone is shown next to the roman numeral V.

II. Function. At this point, the V chord may be preceded or followed by the I chord. The tonic and dominant triads are the basic harmonic building blocks of tonal musical structure and are typically the harmonic goals of the phrase and of larger formal units. The close relationship between the tonic and the dominant derives from their acoustical properties. See the Harmonic Series, Part V, Unit 2. The descending fifth (or ascending fourth) is the strongest relationship in tonal music. See the *circle of fifths*, Part I, Unit 5.

III. Ends of phrases are established by cadences, which articulate points of arrival or rest in the musical flow.

When the progression V–I occurs at the end of a phrase, it is termed an *authentic cadence* (A.C.). When the V chord occurs at the end of a phrase, it is termed a *half cadence* (H.C.). (See Part V, Unit 13.)

IV. At this point, only the root is to be doubled in both the I and the V triads. In any case, doubling the third of the V chord, the leading tone (a *tendency tone*, or tone that tends to move stepwise to a tone of resolution) is to be avoided.

V. There are two basic procedures for the connection of I and V in root position with the root doubled.

A. Common-tone connection.

1. The bass takes the root of the second chord.
2. The common tone is retained in the *same voice* in the second chord.
3. The remaining two upper voices move by conjunct (stepwise) motion to the nearest notes of the second chord. In this connection of V to I, the leading tone normally resolves stepwise to the tonic.

B. Noncommon-tone connection.

1. When the soprano line involves scale-degrees 2-1, 1-2, 3-5, 5-3, or 5-7, the three upper voices normally move contrary to the bass to the nearest notes of the second chord.

d: V♯   i   A: I   V   e: V♯   i

Notice that in this connection of V to I, the leading tone, a tendency tone, does not resolve to tonic, but skips to the dominant. This is known as a *free resolution of the leading tone*. This can occur *only* when the leading tone is in an inner voice.

2. The following is an exceptional procedure to achieve change of spacing when the third of the first chord proceeds to the third of the second chord:

C: V   I   C: I   V   c: i   V♮

VI. See Part V, Unit 4, for definitions and examples of relative and linear motion.

VII. Nonharmonic tones. Any note that is not heard as a member of the prevailing harmony (chord) at any given time is defined as a *nonharmonic (nonchord) tone*. The following are two common types of nonharmonic tones. The passing tone (p.t.) and the auxiliary or neighboring tone (aux. or n.t.) may be either diatonic or chromatic. The illustrations here are diatonic; for chromatic passing tones and auxiliaries, see Part II, Unit 5. Other types of nonharmonic tones will be introduced in subsequent units. Nonharmonic tones may occur simultaneously in more than one voice, in which case they are usually consonant with each other. Excessive nonharmonic activity may obscure the underlying harmonic structure.

A. Passing tone (p.t.). See Part V, Unit 3, for definition.

C: I _____   C: I _____

---

*This exceptional procedure rarely occurs in minor keys because of the diminished fourth between the thirds of the two chords.

Note the use of the ascending form of the melodic minor scale to avoid the melodic augmented second.

B. Auxiliary (aux.) or neighbor tone (n.t.).

Analysis

Look at the examples in Unit 2 of *Music for Analysis*. Refer to Part V, Units 13, 15, and 17. Consider the following:

1. How are harmonies implied melodically?

2. What is the relationship between harmonic and nonharmonic tones in the melodic line?

3. What is the basic shape of the melodic line?

4. How is continuity achieved?

5. What pitches seem structurally important? Why?

6. What types of cadences are used, and where do they occur?

7. How long are the phrases?

8. Are the phrases thematically or motivically related?

9. Do the phrases form a period? Of what type?

Visit the TMM website eWorkbook exercises, online tutorials, and musical examples with audio for this unit are available at the *Techniques and Materials of Music* website, **TMMTheory.com**.

Exercises

The following exercises are to be done on the great staff, employing the tonic and dominant triads in root position.

1. Harmonize the following soprano examples, employing choral open, choral close, or keyboard voicing as indicated:

2. Harmonize the following soprano examples according to the directions for Exercise 1:

3. Add three upper voices to the following basses, using only tonic and dominant root position triads. Work for smooth voice leading, and keep common tones where possible.

4. Realize the following figured basses, using the voicing indicated. Analyze completely, including the roman numerals for all chords and cadence type. Read about figured bass in Part V, Unit 9. The instructor may wish to discuss figured-bass history and practice in more detail. Examples of historical figured basses may be seen in *Music for Analysis*, Part I, Unit 10, and following units. A note in the bass with no figures under it indicates a root position triad (the given note is the root). Any accidental with no number next to it refers to the third (tenth, seventeenth) above the

bass. The natural signs or sharps are needed here to raise the third of the dominant triad (that is, the leading tone). Every accidental in the figures must appear in the music.

A step-by-step demonstration of the procedure for realizing a figured bass can be found on the *Techniques and Materials of Music* website, **TMMTheory.com**. A model can also be found in Part V, Unit 10.

5. Introduce passing tones in the following progressions:

G: I _____   d: i   V♯   A♭:   I   V   f♯:   V♯   i

6. Introduce auxiliaries in the following progressions:

e: i _____   f: V♮   i   A: V _____   e♭:   i   V♮

7. Harmonize the following soprano melodies. Passing tones and auxiliaries may be employed as directed by the instructor. Analyze the cadences. In choral voicing, open or close spacing will be dictated by the register of the soprano, unless otherwise designated by the instructor.

A step-by-step demonstration of the procedure for harmonizing a melody can be found on the *Techniques and Materials of Music* website, **TMMTheory.com**. A model can also be found in Part V, Unit 11.

a.

b.

c.

d.

e.

8. The following patterns may be used for composing melodies, for practice in working with non-harmonic tones, for two voice (soprano and bass) textures, or for improvisation. Be conscious of motivic consistency, direction of line, rhythmic continuity, and clarity of cadence. Refer to Part V, Unit 18, for a discussion of melody. (Note values represent harmonic rhythm.)

A step-by-step demonstration of the procedure for expansion and elaboration of chord formats can be found on the Techniques and Materials of Music website, **TMMTheory.com**. A model can also be found in Part V, Unit 12.

4 The Dominant Seventh Chord in Root Position

C: V7   c: V7

I. The *dominant seventh chord* (V7) consists of a major triad with a minor seventh (Mm7); note the dissonant tritone and minor seventh. In minor keys, the third of the chord (the leading tone) must be raised and indicated by the figured bass accidental in the roman numeral analysis.

II. The V7 functions in the same way as the V, but it occurs infrequently as the cadential chord in a half cadence.

III. Because the V7 is a four-tone chord, all four tones may be present. In many situations the root is doubled and the fifth omitted (see IV–B).

IV. The basic voice-leading rules for connecting I–V apply, with the following observations.

A. Although parallel perfect fifths and perfect octaves are to be avoided, a perfect fifth may move to a diminished fifth if the diminished fifth is subsequently resolved.

C: V   V7   I   V7   V   V7   I   V7   I

B. The voice leading in the progression V7–I is determined by the need to resolve the dissonant intervals. The third and seventh of the V7 are tendency tones. When both tendency tones in the V7 resolve properly, the tritone formed by these tones is resolved. Note that the d5 contracts to a third, and the A4 expands to a sixth. The normal resolution of the seventh is stepwise downward. The third of the chord (the leading tone) resolves to the tonic. The root of the V7 in the bass moves to the root of I. In an incomplete V7, the doubled root remains stationary. This is referred to as the *strict resolution* of the dominant seventh chord.

C: V7   I

At this point, do exercise 1 at the end of this unit.

C. Note that if the tritone of a complete V7 is resolved, the fifth will be omitted and the root tripled in the I. However, when the leading tone is in an *inner voice,* it may skip down a third to the fifth of the I, making both chords complete. As indicated earlier, this is referred to as the *free resolution of the leading tone.*

C: V7   I   V7   I

D. In keyboard voicing only, when the chord seventh is in an inner voice, it frequently moves up a step to the fifth of the I. This is referred to as the *free resolution of the seventh.*

C: V7   I   f: V$^7_\natural$ i

---

*In keyboard voicing, both notes of an implied unison doubling are not commonly written. This results in a momentary reduction to three voices.

E. In the case of chord repetition, the seventh may move from voice to voice. The resolution generally takes place in the last voice in which the seventh appears.

V. The dominant ninth chord (V9).*

A. The V9 consists of a major triad with a minor seventh and a major ninth (MmM9) or a minor seventh and a minor ninth (Mmm9).

B. The V9 is a five-tone chord (when complete) with dominant function. The interval of the ninth is also dissonant and will either be resolved into a dominant seventh prior to resolution to tonic or be resolved directly to the fifth of the I chord. In the former case, the ninth may be understood as a nonharmonic tone. In strict four-part harmony, the fifth is customarily omitted.

---

*The V9 is included here for completeness and because the chord may occur in the musical examples for analysis. For further discussion, refer to Part III, Unit 7.

Analysis

Analyze the examples in Unit 3 of *Music for Analysis*. Refer to Part V, Unit 13, and to the Checklist for Analysis. Consider the following:

1. Where do dominant seventh chords occur? Are they used cadentially?

2. How is the seventh introduced? How is it resolved? Are dominant seventh chords complete or missing the fifth?

3. What types of cadences are used, and where do they occur?

4. How long are the phrases?

5. Are the phrases thematically or motivically related?

6. Do the phrases form a period? Of what type?

 eWorkbook exercises, online tutorials, and musical examples with audio for this unit are available at the *Techniques and Materials of Music* website, **TMMTheory.com**.

Visit the
TMM website

Exercises

1. Resolve the following V7 chords in the given voicing. Indicate the tritone with brackets and resolve strictly, as in IV–B.

2. Resolve the following V7 chords in the given voicing. Indicate the tritone with brackets. Resolve the leading tone or chord seventh freely, whichever is appropriate, as in IV–C and IV–D.

3. Resolve the following V7 chords both strictly and freely, as indicated:

4. Complete the following I–V7 progressions, making the V7 either complete or incomplete, as indicated:

5. Harmonize the following soprano examples in both keyboard and choral voicings, using V7 and I in root position:

A: g: e: E♭:   B:

B♭:   a: f♯:   E: D♭:

A♭:   b: E: d: a:

F: A: f:

c♯:   c:

6. Add three upper voices to the following basses, using only tonic, and dominant triads, and the dominant seventh chord. The 7 beneath a note indicates a root position seventh chord (the other figures, 5 and 3, are implied). The sharp or natural appearing below the note or below the figure 7 in minor-mode examples designates the raised third (tenth, seventeenth) above the bass in the dominant triad or seventh chord. Use a variety of voicings. Work for smooth voice leading and, where possible, contrary motion in the outer voices. Analyze the chords.

7. Harmonize the following melodies, using I, V, and V7 chords in root position. Use the voicing specified by the instructor. Analyze completely, including cadences.

8. Realize the following figured basses. Employ nonharmonic tones. Refer as needed to Part V, Unit 9. Be attentive to the contrapuntal relationship of the outer voices. Analyze completely.

9. Complete the accompaniment to the given melody. Note that the melody contains passing tones.

10. Complete the following in the given two-voice texture.

A step-by-step model for the solution to completion exercises can be found on the *Techniques and Materials of Music* website, **TMMTheory.com**.

Visit the
TMM website

11. The following patterns may be used for composing melodies, for practice in working with various textures, particularly two-voice textures, or for improvisation. Be conscious of motivic consistency, direction of line, rhythmic continuity, and clarity of cadence. Refer to Part V, Unit 12, for a discussion of expansion and elaboration models.

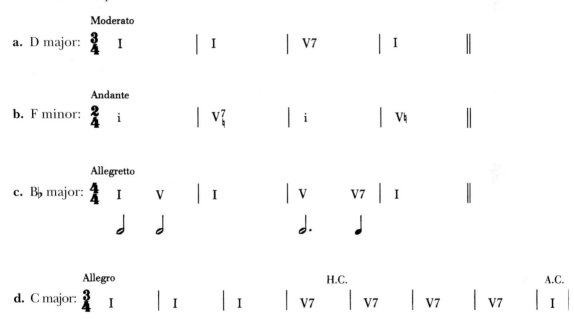

5 Connection of Tonic and Subdominant Triads in Root Position

C: IV   c: iv

I. The roman numerals IV and iv refer to the major and minor triads, respectively, built on the fourth degree of the scale *(subdominant triads)*.

II. Function. The IV chord may be preceded or followed by the I chord. When the I chord is preceded by the IV chord at the end of a phrase, it is termed a *plagal cadence* (P.C.). The ascending fifth relationship is very strong, being the obverse of the dominant-to-tonic descending fifth. See the *circle of fifths*, Part I, Unit 5.

III. The same basic procedures employed in I–V connections are to be employed here.

    A. The common-tone connection procedure is the same for I–V and I–IV connections.

G: I   IV   d: iv   i   a: i   iv

    B. The noncommon-tone connection procedure is the same for I–V and I–IV connections.

B♭: I   IV   g: iv   i   E: IV   I

IV. Nonharmonic tones. Passing tones and auxiliaries may be chromatic.

    A. Passing tone (p.t.). See Part V, Unit 3, for definition.

    B. Auxiliary (aux.) or neighbor tone (n.t.).

 eWorkbook exercises, online tutorials, and musical examples with audio for this unit are available at the *Techniques and Materials of Music* website, **TMMTheory.com**.

Visit the TMM website

Exercises

    1. Harmonize the following soprano examples, employing only the tonic and subdominant triads. Use a variety of voicings and spacings.

2. Add three upper voices to the following basses, employing only the tonic and subdominant triads.

3. Harmonize the following sopranos, employing only the tonic and subdominant triads. Analyze completely.

4. Realize the following figured basses in either keyboard or choral voicing. Analyze completely. Work for smooth voice leading and well-shaped lines.

5. Introduce chromatic passing tones in the following progressions. Analyze completely.

6. Introduce chromatic auxiliaries in the following progressions. Analyze completely.

7. Continue in the given texture for six to eight more measures, ending in a strong cadence. Analyze completely.

Andante grazioso

8. Harmonize and continue for six to twelve more measures in the style of Johann Strauss. Analyze completely.

Allegretto

I_____ V7_____

V7_____ I_____

6 Connection of Subdominant and Dominant Triads in Root Position

I. The IV chord frequently functions as a dominant preparation (predominant) harmony, progressing to V. It rarely follows V. The tonic, subdominant, and dominant triads are often referred to as the "primary triads." The movement from tonic to subdominant to dominant and finally back to tonic typically defines the basic harmonic direction of tonal works and determines form. All other harmonies may be thought of as decorating or substituting for these essential harmonies.

II. The three upper voices move in contrary motion to the bass to the nearest notes of the second chord. (*Note:* In the much rarer progression V–IV, the procedure is the same.)

The following are common connections of IV to V7. Note that the doubled root of the IV may remain stationary, becoming the seventh of the V7.

Analysis

Analyze the examples in Unit 4 of *Music for Analysis*. Refer to Part V, Unit 20, for a discussion of simple forms. In this and all subsequent music discussed in class, consider the following:

1. What is the rate of chord change (harmonic rhythm)?

2. Is it consistent, or does it change at some point in the phrase?

3. Are there motives? Do phrases ever contain two motives? Are these motives shared between the phrases?

4. What is the form of the longer examples? Prepare a simple graph of the form, as suggested in Part V, Unit 20, and label (name) the form.

eWorkbook exercises, online tutorials, and musical examples with audio for this unit are available at the *Techniques and Materials of Music* website, **TMMTheory.com**.

Visit the
TMM website

Exercises

1. Harmonize the following soprano examples, employing only the subdominant and dominant triads and the dominant seventh chord. Use a variety of voicings and spacings.

2. Add three upper voices to the following basses using only tonic, subdominant, and dominant triads, and the dominant seventh chord. Use a variety of voicings. Work for smooth voice leading and, where possible, contrary motion in the outer voices. Analyze the chords.

3. Harmonize the following melodies. Wherever an asterisk occurs, a IV chord is required. Use voicing as specified by the instructor.

a.

b.

c.

d.

4. Realize the following figured basses. Work for smooth voice leading and well-shaped lines. Analyze the chords and scale-degrees in the bass.

a.

b.

c.

5. Complete the following in the given texture:

6. The following patterns may be used for composing melodies, for practice in working with various textures, or for improvisation:

7 Cadences Employing the Tonic, Subdominant, and Dominant Triads in Root Position

Progressions that are used to articulate the ends of phrases (points of arrival or rest in the musical flow) are termed *cadences*. For a complete discussion of cadences, see Part V, Unit 13. Tonal music is built around these tonic and dominant arrival points, and they form one of the fundamental building blocks of musical structure.

I. A *perfect authentic cadence* (P.A.C.), or full cadence, employs the progression V (or V7)–I, with the first scale-degree in the soprano in the I chord. Both chords must be in root position.

A perfect authentic cadence is the strongest cadence and is used to mark important formal junctures in the music, such as the ends of sections or periods.

II. An *imperfect authentic cadence* (I.A.C.) employs the progression V (or V7)–I, with the third or fifth scale-degree in the soprano in the I chord.

An imperfect authentic cadence is weaker than a P.A.C. and signifies both harmonic arrival and likely continuation. Thus, it may be used as the medial cadence in a period and at those junctures where the composer wishes to establish a weaker sense of closure.

III. A *half cadence* (H.C), or semi-cadence, employs a progression ending on V.

C: I   V   d: i   V♯   C: IV   V   d: iv   V♯

A half cadence is a relatively weak event, requiring continuation, because it is harmonically open-ended.

IV. A *plagal cadence* (P.C.) employs the progression IV–I.

A: IV   I   f: iv   i

A plagal cadence is generally a terminal cadence and indicates closure. It often follows a perfect authentic cadence.

Analysis

Analyze music assigned by the instructor. In addition to the items included to this point, consider the following:

1. What types of cadences are used, and where do they occur?

2. How long are the phrases?

3. Are the phrases related?

4. Do the phrases form a period? Of what type?

 eWorkbook exercises, online tutorials, and musical examples with audio for this unit are available at the *Techniques and Materials of Music* website, **TMMTheory.com**.

Visit the
TMM website

Exercises

1. Harmonize the following cadential basses and sopranos. Use a variety of voicings and spacings. Analyze the scale-degrees in the soprano.

2. Cadential soprano lines. Harmonize in four voices, using a variety of voicings. Analyze chords and scale-degrees in the soprano.

3. Cadential bass lines. Harmonize in four voices, using a variety of voicings. Analyze chords and scale-degrees in the bass.

4. Realize the following figured basses. Work for smooth voice leading and well-shaped lines. Analyze completely.

5. Construct the following cadence formulas:

P.A.C. in E minor	P.A.C. in A♭ major
H.C. in B♭ major	P.C. in D minor
P.C. in A minor	I.A.C. in G major
I.A.C. in F♯ minor	H.C. in C♯ minor
H.C. in B♭ minor	P.A.C. in E major

6. Compose four-measure phrases ending with the following cadence formulas. Employ textures specified by the instructor. Be attentive to harmonic rhythm, motivic consistency, and rhythmic continuity.

P.A.C. in D major

H.C. in G minor

I.A.C. in E♭ major

P.C. in B major

7. Compose an eight-measure period for piano, the first phrase ending with an H.C. and the second with a P.A.C. Edit fully and specifically, including tempo, phrasing, and dynamics. (*Note*: The following units in Part V will be helpful: Unit 11, Unit 13, and Unit 17.)

8 The Cadential Tonic Six-Four Chord

C: $\left[\text{I}_4^6\right]$ c: $\left[\text{i}_4^6\right]$

I. The *tonic six-four chord* (I_4^6) is a triad in *second inversion,* a triad arranged so that its fifth is in the bass; note the intervals of the sixth and fourth above the lowest note. The fourth in this context is a dissonant interval.

II. In common usage most six-four chords are considered nonfunctional *(linear),* since the tones in the upper voices can be analyzed as nonharmonic. The cadential tonic six-four chord usually immediately precedes the V or V7 at an authentic or half cadence, and the sixth and fourth above the bass function as melodic embellishments to tones of the dominant, most frequently appoggiaturas, passing tones, or suspensions. (See Part V, Unit 3 for definitions of nonharmonic tones.) Even though the cadential six-four chord is comprised of notes forming the tonic chord it represents dominant function. There are three ways in which this usage may be analyzed. (Note that linear chords are analyzed in brackets, and their type of use is indicated. Other linear six-four chords are discussed in Part II, Unit 12.)

    A. Nonharmonic tones

D: I   V—————   I

B. Linear chord

I   cad.
[I$^6_4$]   V   I

C. Incorporating figured bass

I   V $^6_4$ — $^5_3$ I

III. Because the cadential six-four chord represents dominant function, the fifth of the chord (that note in the bass and the root of the dominant chord) is doubled.

C: [I$^6_4$]

IV. Voice leading.

  A. The following occur in normal resolution.

    1. The bass remains stationary.

    2. The intervals of the sixth and fourth above the bass move stepwise downward.

    3. The doubled fifth may remain stationary or move to the seventh of the V7.

    4. The chord is metrically stronger than the chord of resolution.

B. When resolution is to V7, the sixth above the bass may move up stepwise to the chord seventh. This generally occurs when the sixth is in an inner voice.

Analysis

Analyze the examples in Unit 5 of *Music for Analysis*. Refer to Part V, Unit 13, and to the Checklist for Analysis (Part V, Unit 21). Bring further examples from the literature into class.

1. What types of cadences are used, and where do they occur?

2. How long are the phrases?

3. Are the phrases thematically or motivically related?

4. Do the phrases form a period? Of what type?

eWorkbook exercises, online tutorials, and musical examples with audio for this unit are available at the *Techniques and Materials of Music* website, **TMMTheory.com**.

Visit the
TMM website

Exercises

1. Harmonize the following sopranos in a variety of voicings and spacings; use tonic six-four chords where indicated by an asterisk:

2. Realize the following figured basses.

3. Harmonize the following melodies, employing tonic six-four chords where indicated by the asterisks. Analyze completely.

4. Realize the following figured basses. Remember that the figure $\frac{6}{4}$ designates a triad in second inversion. Analyze completely.

5. Continue the harmonization of the given melody in the texture and style indicated by the opening bars. Use the complete harmonic vocabulary studied to date, and include at least one cadential six-four chord. Score your results for instruments available in class. Information on ranges and transpositions can be found in Part V, Unit 23; explanation and examples for analysis of chordal textures can be found in Part V, Unit 17.

Alla Britannia

6. Compose an original chorale for either instruments or chorus consisting of an eight-bar period, the first phrase ending on a half cadence and the second phrase ending on a perfect authentic cadence. Edit fully. Units 13 and 23 of Part V will be helpful.

7. The following patterns may be used for composition or improvisation:

    a. D major:

    b. G minor:

    c. D♭ major:

9 Tonic, Subdominant, and Dominant Triads in First Inversion

C: I6   IV6   V6

I. A chord in *first inversion* (sixth chord) is one arranged so that its third is in the bass. The 6 beside the roman numeral in the analysis indicates that the root is a sixth above the bass. Refer to Part V, Unit 9, for further discussion of figured-bass symbols.

II. A chord in first inversion has the same function as that chord in root position. The final chord of a cadence is rarely in inversion. A V6–I progression at a cadence point forms an imperfect authentic cadence. (See Part V, Unit 13.)

III. Doubling.

    A. Root doubling is preferable.

G: I6   IV6   V6

In keyboard voicings, unison doublings are often implicit rather than written out.

G: I6   IV6

B. Fifth doubling is next in preference.

C. Third doubling is the least preferable (in the V chord, the leading tone is not to be doubled).

D. Normally all sixth chords are complete.

IV. As with progressions of triads in root position, smoothness of line is a major consideration in first inversion. Thus, progression to the nearest appropriate spacing and doubling of the succeeding chord is the normal procedure in voice leading.

V. The need for a more melodic bass line results in the use of chords in first inversion. Some characteristic bassline patterns are illustrated below. Careted numbers indicate scale degrees in the bass. Observe which note of the chord is doubled.

A. I6

B. IV6

1. A IV6 chord used to resolve a V or V7 chord is called a *deceptive resolution.* When this progression occurs at the end of a phrase, the resulting cadence is called a *deceptive cadence (D.C.).* Other possibilities for deceptive resolutions will be found in later units.

2. The progression iv6–V in a minor key, when used as a terminal progression, is sometimes called a *phrygian cadence*. It is typically used in Baroque compositions to close a middle movement of a larger work.

c: iv6   V♮
      ^6   ^5

e: iv6   V♯
      ^6   ^5

C. V6. In the following examples, note that successive first-inversion chords require a change of doubling or spacing to avoid parallel fifths and/or octaves.

C: I   V6   I   V6   I   I   V6   IV6   [I⁶₄]   V   V   IV6   V6   I
    ^8 ^7   ^8 ^7   ^8 ^8 ^7   ^6   ^5   ^5 ^6 ^7   ^8

D. Temporary reduction to three-voice texture for consecutive sixth chords is typical of keyboard writing.

C: V   IV6   V6   I
     ^5   ^6   ^7   ^8

VI. The following example incorporates the most common first-inversion idioms. Note the bass scale-degrees associated with these idioms.

C: I   I6   IV   V   IV6   V6   I
    ^1   ^3   ^4   ^5   ^6   ^7   ^8

VII. At this point it is advisable to study the guidelines for voice leading and doubling in Part V, Units 5 and 6.

VIII. Although root doubling is most common, the fifth, and more rarely the third, may be doubled in I, IV, and V chords in root position to facilitate smoothness of line. The leading tone, however, should not be doubled. See example V–C above.

IX. Nonharmonic tones (see Part V, Unit 3, for descriptions).

A. Escape tone (e.t.).

B. Free neighbor (f.n.) or incomplete neighbor tone.

C. Anticipation (ant.).

Analysis

Analyze the examples in Unit 6 of *Music for Analysis*. In this and all subsequent music discussed in class, consider the following, and refer to Part V, Unit 19, for a discussion of counterpoint.

1. What is the contrapuntal relationship between the outer voices?

2. Is the bass primarily functional or linear?

3. Does imitation occur within the texture?

 eWorkbook exercises, online tutorials, and musical examples with audio for this unit are available at the *Techniques and Materials of Music* website, **TMMTheory.com**.

Visit the
TMM website

Exercises

1. Realize the following figured basses, employing triads in first inversion as indicated:

2. In the following progressions, introduce escape tones where indicated by an asterisk:

3. In the following progressions, introduce free neighbors where indicated by an asterisk:

4. In the following progressions, introduce anticipations where indicated by an asterisk:

5. Harmonize the following melodies, employing triads in first inversion where appropriate. Employ nonharmonic tones. Strive for a musical bass line, being attentive to the counterpoint between the outer voices. Analyze all work completely.

a.

b.

6. Realize the following figured basses. Employ nonharmonic tones. Work for a musical soprano melody, being attentive to the counterpoint between the outer voices. Analyze all work completely. For an explanation of figured-bass symbols, refer to Part V, Unit 9; refer to Part V, Unit 10, for the procedure in harmonizing a figured bass. Some of these basses may be worked out in two- or three-voice contrapuntal texture, as indicated by the instructor; no imitation is required. See Part V, Unit 19, for a discussion of counterpoint.

A step-by-step demonstration of the procedure for realizing a figured bass can be found on the *Techniques and Materials of Music* website, **TMMTheory.com**. A model can also be found in Part V, Unit 10.

7. Study examples of ground bass (*basso ostinato*) from the literature, and compose a passacaglia using the following ground bass. Refer to Part V, Unit 19, for a discussion of counterpoint.

8. Complete the following two-voice contrapuntal exercises.

A step-by-step demonstration of a possible solution to a contrapuntal exercises can be found on the *Techniques and Materials of Music* website, **TMMTheory.com**.

a.

b.

(unfigured)

9. Harmonize the following unfigured basses. Employ triads in first inversion where appropriate, supplying figures and analyzing completely. Work for a musical soprano melody, being attentive to the counterpoint between the outer voices.

10 The Supertonic Triad

C: ii   ii6   c: ii°   ii°6

I. The *supertonic triad* is a minor triad in the major mode and a diminished triad (indicated by the symbol °) in the minor mode. It is found more often in first inversion than in root position, especially in the minor mode.

II. Function. The supertonic triad will generally function as a dominant preparation, a progression analogous to IV–V. The supertonic triad may be understood as a quasidominant to the dominant, the descending fifth relationship corresponding to that from dominant to tonic. See the *circle of fifths*, Part I, Unit 5.

III. Doubling.

    A. ii in root position: Doubled root is preferable, and third or fifth is next.

    B. ii in first inversion: Doubled third is preferable, and root or fifth is next.

    C. ii° and ii°6: Doubled third is preferable; the root is doubled occasionally, but never the fifth.

IV. The supertonic triad may be preceded by tonic or subdominant chords.

    A. When moving from tonic to supertonic, both in root position, upper voices generally move contrary to the bass, but the third of the I may move to the third of the ii.

C: I   ii   a: i   ii°

    B. When moving from subdominant to supertonic, both in root position, hold the common tones.

C: IV   ii   A: IV   ii

C. When either chord is in inversion, move in the smoothest way.

F: I   ii6   e: iv   ii°6   E♭:   I   ii6   a: i6   ii°6

V. Connection of the supertonic triad with V and V7.

A. Supertonic triad in root position.

1. The bass moves from the root of ii to the root of V.
2. Upper voices move in contrary motion to the nearest chord tone.
3. The third of ii may remain stationary, becoming the seventh of V7.
4. The fifth of ii° in the minor mode is a tendency tone, usually resolving downward to the root of V.

C: ii   V   e: ii°   V♯   B♭:   ii   V   A: ii   V7   B♭   ii $\left[\text{I}\begin{smallmatrix}6\\4\end{smallmatrix}\right]$ V

5. The common tone connection can be used only when the quality of the ii is minor. A doubled root allows one tone to leap to the seventh of the V7 or remain stationary.

E♭:   ii   V   E♭:   ii   V7   D: ii   V7   I   D: ii   V   I

B. Supertonic triad in first inversion.

    1. Voice leading is analogous to the IV–V progression. Note the doubling; here again, a doubled root may leap or remain stationary.

    2. Common tone connection in major mode.

    3. In the common tone connection in minor mode, note that the fifth of the supertonic triad must resolve down to avoid the melodic augmented second.

VI. The seventh chord built on the supertonic has the same function as the supertonic triad. This chord will be fully discussed in Part II, Unit 17.

Analysis

Analyze the examples in Unit 7 of *Music for Analysis*. Bring other examples from the literature into class.

eWorkbook exercises, online tutorials, and musical examples with audio for this unit are available at the *Techniques and Materials of Music* website, **TMMTheory.com**.

Visit the
TMM website

Exercises

1. Harmonize the following sopranos in both keyboard and choral voicing:

   a. Use ii in root position where indicated by the asterisk.

   b. Use ii in first inversion where indicated by the asterisk.

2. Realize the following figured basses, employing nonharmonic tones where appropriate. Strive for a musical melody line, and analyze all work completely. Some of these may be worked out in two- or three-voice contrapuntal texture.

3. Harmonize the following melodies. Work for a musical bass line, and analyze all work completely. Refer to Part V, Units 8 and 11, for discussions of chord functions and harmonizing a melody.

a.

b.

c.

d.

4. Complete the following in the given texture:

5. Complete the following contrapuntal exercises:

a.

b.

6. The following patterns may be used for composition or improvisation:

a. B major: ¢ I | I | ii6 | V̇ | ii | ii | V | I ‖

b. E minor:

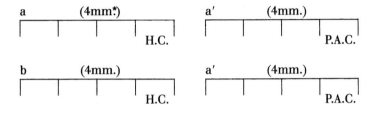

7. Compose a piece using the following phrase design: a   a′   b   a′

a   (4mm.*)
H.C.

a′   (4mm.)
P.A.C.

b   (4mm.)
H.C.

a′   (4mm.)
P.A.C.

---

*mm. = measures.

11 Inversions of the Dominant Seventh Chord

I. In the inversions of the dominant seventh chord, the tritone is resolved in the same manner as the root position dominant seventh chord.

A. In the first inversion, V^6_5, the third is in the bass; figures represent the intervals of the root (6) and seventh (5) above the bass.

B. In the second inversion, V^4_3, the fifth is in the bass; figures represent the intervals of the root (4) and seventh (3) above the bass. The figure $\cancel{6}$ is normally used only in the minor mode to indicate alteration of the leading tone. A slash through a figure means that the note is to be raised a half step.

_____

*Note the doubled third, which often occurs in the resolution of the V^4_3.

Note the exceptional resolution of the seventh in the progression I–V$^4_3$–I6, resulting from parallel tenths in the bass and soprano.

C. In the third inversion, V$^{(4)}_2$ the seventh is in the bass; the figure represents the interval of the root above the bass (2). The figure 4 is normally used only in the minor mode to indicate the alteration of the leading tone.

D. The fifth may be omitted and the root doubled in the V$^6_5$ and the V2.

<hr />

*Note the doubled fifth.

E. The following example includes several very common inverted dominant seventh chord idioms, shown bracketed. Note the bass scale-degrees associated with these idioms.

II. Non-harmonic tones (see Part V, Unit 3, for descriptions).

In both the appoggiatura (app.) and the suspension (sus.), the note of resolution should not be doubled unless it is normally doubled in the chord of resolution. It is helpful to observe that the appoggiatura and suspension are similar except that the suspension is prepared.

A. Appoggiatura.

Appoggiaturas may also be chromatic.

B. Suspension.

C: I   V   I   V   C: V7   I   V7   I

Analysis

Analyze the examples in Unit 8 of *Music for Analysis*. Refer to Part V, Unit 20, for a discussion of small forms. In addition to all elements previously discussed, consider the following:

1. Where do inversions of the dominant seventh occur? What is the nature of the bass line at that point? Analyze the bass line with scale-degree numbers.

2. Do inversions of V7 occur at cadence points?

eWorkbook exercises, online tutorials, and musical examples with audio for this unit are available at the *Techniques and Materials of Music* website, **TMMTheory.com**.

Visit the
TMM website

Exercises

1. Harmonize the following, employing inversions of the dominant seventh as indicated:

G: V2   F: V$_5^6$ D♭: V$_3^4$ C: V$_5^6$ E♭:   V2

B♭:   V2   g: V$_5^6$ a: V$_4^6$$_3$ b: V$_2^4$ f: V$_5^6$

2. In the following progressions, introduce appoggiaturas where indicated by an asterisk:

d: i   V♯   A: V7   I   E♭: IV   I   G: V   I

3. In the following progressions, introduce suspensions where indicated by an asterisk:

b: i   V♯   A♭: I   ii6   A: IV   V7   g: V⁶₅   i

4. Realize the following figured basses. Employ nonharmonic tones. Work for a musical soprano melody, being attentive to the counterpoint between the outer voices. Analyze all work completely. Refer to Part V, Unit 9, for a discussion of figured-bass symbols and Part V, Unit 10, for a discussion of harmonizing a figured bass.

a.

b.

c.

d.

e.

f.

d: 6   6   6   #   6   #   4   6   6   7
    5   4   2   4   #
        3

5. Harmonize the following melodies, employing inversions of the dominant seventh chord in places marked with an asterisk. Employ nonharmonic tones. Work for a musical bass line, being attentive to the counterpoint between the outer voices. Refer to Part V, Units 8 and 11, for a discussion of chord functions and harmonizing a melody.

a.

b.

Allegretto

c.

Moderato

d.

Nicht zu schnell

e.

Andante

6. Complete the following to a total length of at least eight measures. Continuing with the given texture, score the example for instruments that are available in class. Refer to Part V, Unit 23, for information on instrumental ranges and transpositions.

7. Realize the following figured basses in the given contrapuntal textures:

a.

b.

8. Study examples of ground bass (basso ostinato) from the literature. Then compose a passacaglia for organ using the following unfigured bass. Refer to Part V, Unit 19, on counterpoint.

9. In the style of Exercise 6, compose a contrasting period of eight to sixteen measures. End the first phrase with a half cadence and the second with a perfect authentic cadence.

10. The following patterns may be used for composition or improvisation:

11. Compose a brief binary composition, using the following formal outline:

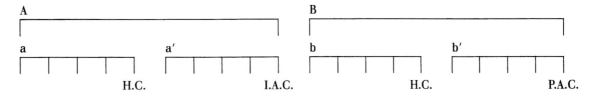

Linear (Embellishing) Six-Four and Other Chords

12

I. Many chord structures may be analyzed as the simultaneous use of several nonharmonic tones. Often the resulting chord structure is recognizable as a particular type of chord (triad, seventh chord, and so forth) but because of its melodic origins is analyzed as a *linear chord*. This is indicated by placing the roman numeral in brackets along with the designation of the type of nonharmonic use (for example, *n.c.* for *neighboring chord* and *p.c.* for *passing chord*). Included in this category are the various embellishing six-four chords. These chords can also be analyzed simply as a combination of nonharmonic tones. The following idioms are particularly common.

A. Neighboring (auxiliary or pedal) chords.

1. The bass remains stationary.
2. The upper voices move to neighbors and back. Occasionally one or more upper voices may have passing tones, as in the last example that follows.
3. The chord generally appears on a weak beat or part of a beat.

B. Passing chords.

1. The bass moves conjunctly, generally connecting a root-position chord with a first-inversion chord.
2. The chord appears on a weak beat or part of a beat.

C. With appoggiatura or suspension chords, voice leading is analogous to the cadential I$_4^6$, and the chord generally occurs on a strong beat or part of a beat.

D. Six-four chords may occur as a result of an arpeggiated bass line, with a bass line that alternates between root and fifth in many accompanimental patterns, or when the melody is in the bass.

II. Any chord may be functional or linear, depending on the context. Chords that lack a functional root relationship with the preceding and following chords are often best analyzed as linear. This situation frequently arises with a highly conjunct bass line.

Analysis

Analyze music assigned by the instructor. Refer to the Checklist for Analysis (Part V, Unit 21).

 eWorkbook exercises, online tutorials, and musical examples with audio for this unit are available at the *Techniques and Materials of Music* website, **TMMTheory.com**.

Visit the
TMM website

Exercises

1. Realize the following figured basses, paying particular attention to the shape and direction of the melodic line. Analyze completely.

   a.

   b.

2. Harmonize the following melodies, using six-four chords where indicated by an asterisk. Analyze completely.

   a.

   b.

3. Complete the harmonization of the following melody in the given texture. Use linear chords wherever appropriate.

4. Harmonize the following melodies. Tones with asterisks may be treated as simple melodic embellishments (nonharmonic tones) or "harmonized" with other nonharmonic embellishing tones. The resultant sonorities may be analyzed as linear chords. In these melodies and all subsequent melodies with embellishing tones, use the *slowest harmonic rhythm* appropriate to the tempo and character of the melody.

a.

13 Submediant and Mediant Triads in Root Position and First Inversion

C: vi   vi6   iii   iii6   c: VI   VI6   III   III6

I. The roman numerals VI and vi refer to the major and minor triads built on the sixth degree of the scale (*submediant triads*). The roman numerals III and iii refer to the major and minor triads built on the third degree of the scale (*mediant triads*).

II. Function. The submediant and mediant triads are used less frequently than the primary triads (I, IV, and V) and have less significance for the building of musical structure. They may be thought of as embellishing or substituting for the more fundamental harmonies. They are often found in sequences.

Progressions.

A. The VI chord is usually preceded by III, I, or V and is usually followed by II, V, or IV.

C: I   vi   ii6   V   bb: i   VI   V♮

B. V–VI or V7–VI is a deceptive resolution. When this progression occurs at a cadence point, it is termed a *deceptive cadence (D.C.)*. Note the usual resolution of the leading tone and the seventh of the dominant seventh chord, as well as the resulting doubled third in the submediant.

C: V7   vi   c: V♮7   VI   C: V7   vi

C. The III chord is usually preceded by I or VI and is usually followed by IV or VI. Note the scale-degree formulas in the upper voice associated with these progressions.

III. Linear uses.

A. The root position VI chord can be used to embellish the I chord.

B. Both VI6 and III6 are weak structures; they are rarely independent.

In these instances the mediant and submediant may be understood as linear chords, or the third or sixth scale-degree may be understood as a nonharmonic tone.

C. In minor, a sonority that may look like III+6 is normally heard and used as a V, with scale-degree 3 as a nonharmonic tone. The root position III+ is usually the result of a chromatic passing tone.

For a further discussion of the augmented III, see Part II, Unit 15.

Analysis

Analyze music containing phrases of irregular length.

1. Are the phrases shorter or longer than normal?

2. What devices are used to achieve this irregularity?

3. Do the phrases form periodic or phrase-group relationships?

eWorkbook exercises, online tutorials, and musical examples with audio for this unit are available at the *Techniques and Materials of Music* website, **TMMTheory.com**.

Visit the
TMM website

Exercises

1. Realize the following figured basses. (Refer to Part V, Unit 10.) Employ nonharmonic tones, and work for a musical soprano melody. Analyze all work completely.

2. Harmonize the following melodies, employing mediant and submediant triads where appropriate:

a.

Largo

b.

Moderato assai

c.

Andantino

d.

Allegretto

e.

Moderato

vi

3. Study examples of nonimitative two-voice counterpoint in *Music for Analysis*. Then, complete the following exercises and analyze completely, being attentive to the rhythmic and intervallic relationships between the voices and to the clarity of the harmonic implications. Refer to Part V, Unit 19, on counterpoint.

a.

b.

4. Add a bass voice to the given melody. The added voice should be as melodically independent as possible.

5. Compose a period for an instrumental combination available in class, employing the phrase and cadence structure outlined here. (Refer to Part V, Unit 23, for information on instrumental ranges and transpositions.)

6. The following patterns may be used for composition or improvisation:

a. D major:

b. E minor:

7. Compose a double period for an instrumental combination available in class, employing the period, phrase, and cadence structure outlined here. (Refer to Part V, Unit 23, for information on instrumental ranges and transposition.)

14 The Leading-Tone Triad

C: vii°   vii°6   c: vii°   vii°⌀

I. The *leading-tone triad* is a diminished triad; it occurs in both major and minor modes.

II. The chord is used with dominant function except to replace V at a half cadence. It may also be used as a linear (embellishing) chord (still associated with tonic harmony). The triad is almost always in first inversion; root position is very rare, and second inversion is virtually never used.

III. The third is usually doubled, as the root and fifth are tendency tones.

IV. Voice leading.

    A. The root of the chord (the leading tone) always resolves stepwise upward.

    B. One third of the chord generally moves stepwise downward, whereas the other third moves stepwise upward in contrary motion.

    C. The fifth of the chord, though a tendency tone, typically is freely resolved, moving stepwise up to the fifth of the tonic chord. However, see the third example that follows, in which the tritone in the outer voices resolves.

e:	i	[vii°⌀]	i6	B♭:	IV	vii°6	I	F:	IV6	vii°	I
scale-degrees:	1̂	2̂	3̂		4̂	2̂	1̂		6̂	7̂	8̂

G: I   vii°6   I6
      1̂   2̂   3̂

V. A complete summary of part-writing and doubling procedures will be found in Part V, Units 5, 6, and 7.

Analysis

Analyze music assigned by the instructor, keeping in mind all the elements previously considered.

eWorkbook exercises, online tutorials, and musical examples with audio for this unit are available at the *Techniques and Materials of Music* website, **TMMTheory.com**.

Visit the
TMM website

Exercises

1. Realize the following figured and unfigured basses, using nonharmonic tones where appropriate:

a.

b.

c.

d.

2. Harmonize the following melodies. Three- or four-voice instrumental or keyboard textures may be employed. Analyze all work completely.

a.

Andantino

b.

Moderato

c.

d.

3. Complete the following fragment in the indicated texture for instruments available in class. Information on ranges and transpositions can be found in Part V, Unit 23; explanation and examples for analysis of three-part texture can be found in Part V, Unit 17.

4. Complete the following in the given contrapuntal textures:

a.

b.

5. The following patterns may be used for composition or improvisation:

15 Variant Qualities of Triads

I. Scalar variants.

    A. The following are variants relating to use of the melodic minor scale. Note that these chords use either the raised form of scale-degree 6 or the subtonic. The figured-bass symbols for the altered notes must be placed next to the roman numeral in the analysis.

    IV, ii, and vi° are found with the ascending form of the scale; v is found with the descending form.

    B. The presence of the third scale-degree as a nonharmonic tone over dominant harmony will give the effect of an augmented III + 6. Such sonorities are best understood as V, with the third scale-degree analyzed as nonharmonic.

116

C. Occasionally a triad will appear over the subtonic in the minor mode (unaltered seventh scale-degree of natural minor). The major triad that results is associated either with a major III chord (with the effect of a momentary shift to the relative major) or with bass motion passing stepwise down from the tonic note. Note that the voice leading in the progression VII–III is analogous to the progression V–I in the relative major and can be analyzed as V/III-III (see Part III, Unit 1).

The progression VII–III often occurs as part of a circle-of-fifths harmonic sequence.

Analysis

Analyze the examples of music using scalar variants in Unit 12 of *Music for Analysis*. Refer to the Checklist for Analysis (Part V, Unit 21).

Exercises

1. Write the following chords in root position, using only the treble staff. Add the appropriate accidentals to the roman numerals.

f: v, ii, VII, IV, vi°

c#: IV, ii, VII, v, IV

2. Harmonize the following soprano lines, using scalar variants where appropriate:

3. Realize the following figured basses:

4. Realize the following figured basses:

a.

b.

c.

d.

5. Harmonize the following melodies, using the variant triads discussed in this unit. Analyze completely.

a.

b.

c.

Allegro

d.

Maestoso

II. Modal borrowing (interchange of mode, modal mixture).

> **A.** The modal scale-degrees (those which distinguish a major key from its parallel minor) are 3, 6, and 7. For expressive or coloristic reasons, composers sometimes employ modal scale-degrees "borrowed" from the parallel key, usually associated with chords borrowed from that key. The function of these chords remains the same. Such borrowed chords are most often found in works in the major mode, and thus come from the parallel minor key. They may be analyzed with the symbol "M.B." and the appropriate roman numeral, with care taken to show the proper chord quality. Note in the following examples the accidentals required in the figured bass.

modal degrees

tonal degrees

B. Modally borrowed chords may replace or follow the diatonic version of the same chord. They rarely precede the diatonic version.

C. A work in the minor mode may end on a major tonic triad. The raised third of this chord is called the *Picardy third (tierce de Picardie)*. This is the most common borrowing from the parallel major mode.

Analysis

Analyze the examples of music using modal borrowing in Unit 12 of *Music for Analysis*. Refer to the Checklist for Analysis (Part V, Unit 21).

Visit the
TMM website

eWorkbook exercises, online tutorials, and musical examples with audio for this unit are available at the *Techniques and Materials of Music* website, **TMMTheory.com**.

Exercises

1. a. Analyze the following modally borrowed chords. Include roman numerals and figured bass with proper accidentals.

b. Alter the following chords by modal borrowing. Analyze both chords of each pair with roman numerals and figured-bass symbols, including accidentals.

2. Write the following chords in root position, using only the treble staff. Add the appropriate accidentals to the roman numerals.

D: III, iv, i, VI, ii°

A♭: VII, III, ii°, iv, i

3. Harmonize the following soprano lines in four voices, using modal borrowing where appropriate. Analyze.

a.

b.

c.

d.

4. Realize the following figured basses:

a.

b.

c.

d.

5. Complete the accompaniment to the following melody in the given texture and style. Use modally borrowed chords where appropriate.

6. The following patterns may be used for composition or improvisation:

16 The Sequence

I. A *sequence (seq.)* is the repetition of a musical motive or pattern on successively higher or lower pitch levels. Refer to Part V, Unit 16, for further explanation and examples.

II. Sequential progressions.

A. Sequences may employ functional progressions. When all the diatonic triads occur in this context, the IV and the vii will not have their more usual functions.

B. The melodic pattern may take precedence over harmonic function, resulting in a linear progression. In this case, the harmonies preceding and following the sequence will be functional.

III. Sequences generally involve a minimum of two and a maximum of four statements of the sequential unit.

Analysis

Look at music containing sequences.

1. What is the sequential unit?

2. How many times is it stated?

3. By what interval is it transposed?

4. What type of progression is employed?

eWorkbook exercises, online tutorials, and musical examples with audio for this unit are available at the *Techniques and Materials of Music* website, **TMMTheory.com**.

Visit the TMM website

Exercises

1. Continue the given patterns in each sequence. Conclude each pattern with an appropriate cadence, and analyze all work completely. The sequential unit is bracketed, and the first transposition is established.

2. Harmonize the following melodies containing sequences:

a.

b.

c.

d.

3. Realize the following figured and unfigured basses using contrapuntal textures if desired. Employ sequence in the upper voices where the bass is sequential.

A step-by-step demonstration of the procedure for realizing a figured bass can be found on the *Techniques and Materials of Music* website, **TMMTheory.com**. A model can also be found in Part V, Unit 10.

a.

b.

4. Complete the following in the indicated texture:

a.

5. Use the following patterns as the basis for sequential elaboration. The progressions may be written out using a variety of textures or improvised using keyboard alone or keyboard with instruments.

6. Compose original melodies employing sequential patterns, and harmonize accordingly. These examples may be written for piano or for instruments available in class.

17 The Supertonic Seventh Chord

C: ii7   c: ii°7

I. In the major mode the *supertonic seventh chord* is a minor triad with a minor seventh (mm7 or m7), commonly termed a *minor seventh chord*. In the minor mode it is a diminished triad with a minor seventh (dm7), commonly termed a *half-diminished seventh chord* (indicated by the symbol°). The ii°7 is often found as a borrowed chord in the major mode.

II. A supertonic seventh chord normally resolves to V or V7.

III. Voice leading.

    A. Supertonic to dominant.

        1. The chord seventh resolves stepwise downward.
        2. The fifth moves stepwise downward or skips to the seventh of the V7.
        3. The third may skip down or remain stationary, becoming the seventh of the V7. In first inversion the third moves stepwise upward to the root of the V.
        4. The root moves to the root of V or remains stationary.

129

| g: | ii°$^4_2$ | V$^6_5$ | i | G: | I | ii7 | V |

B. The linear ii7 chord may occur as a neighboring or a passing chord. The second example that follows is a characteristic three-voice progression occurring most frequently in keyboard textures:

		n.c.				p.c.	
a:	i	[ii°$^6_5$]	i	or	Bb:	I	[ii7]	I6
					Bb:	I	___

C. A plagal cadence may employ the progression ii$^6_5$–I:

| F: | ii $^6_5$ | I | | b: | ii°$^6_5$ | i |

Analysis

Analyze the examples in Unit 13 of *Music for Analysis*. Be sure to consider the underlying structural elements, as well as the surface detail.

eWorkbook exercises, online tutorials, and musical examples with audio for this unit are available at the *Techniques and Materials of Music* website, **TMMTheory.com**.

Visit the
TMM website

---

*Here the third is doubled (and the fifth omitted) to avoid parallel fifths from I to ii7.

Exercises

1. Harmonize the following sopranos in both keyboard and choral voicing. Use a ii7 wherever indicated by an asterisk. Use a variety of inversions as well as root position; some of the inversions are indicated. Analyze completely.

a.

b.

c.

d.

(keyboard voicing only)

2. Realize the following figured basses:

a.

b.

c.

3. Complete the realization of the following figured bass in the given texture. Then, compose an *espressivo* solo line for an instrument available in class.

4. Complete the following in the given contrapuntal textures:

a.

(unfigured)

b.

5. Compose a solo for voice with piano accompaniment using a brief three- or four-line poem in the form a a′ b. Refer to Part V, Unit 20, for a discussion of bar form.

6. The following patterns may be used for composition or improvisation:

a. D minor:

Allegro

$\mathbf{C}$ i | i | ii$^{\sharp 4}_{2}$ | ii$^{\sharp 4}_{2}$ | V$^{6}_{5}$ | V$^{7}_{\sharp}$ | ii$^{\sharp 6}_{5}$ V$^{7}_{\sharp}$ | i ‖

b. G major:

Siciliano

$^{3}_{8}$ I | I | ii$^{6}_{5}$ | V | V | vi | ii$^{6}_{5}$ V7 | I ‖

18 The Leading-Tone Seventh Chord

I. A seventh chord built on the seventh scale-degree is a *leading-tone seventh chord.*

A. In the minor mode it is a diminished triad with a diminished seventh (dd7), commonly termed a *fully diminished seventh (vii° 7).*

1. The root of the vii°7 is always the *raised* form of the seventh scale-degree (the leading tone).

2. The chord is always fully diminished.

B. In the major mode it is a diminished triad with a diminished seventh (dd7), or a diminished triad with a minor seventh (dm7), commonly termed a *half-diminished seventh* (vii°7).

1. The chord can be either fully or half diminished.

2. The fully diminished seventh requires that the sixth scale-degree (seventh of the chord) be lowered chromatically. This may be understood as a modally borrowed chord.

II. The leading-tone seventh chord has a dominant function. It may be used in place of a dominant triad or seventh chord, although it is rarely used as the final chord of a half cadence.

III. Normal resolution is to a tonic triad. Because the root, fifth, and seventh are tendency tones, their resolution is usually strictly observed.

A. For the fully diminished seventh, the seventh resolves down by step, the fifth resolves down by step, the third resolves up or down, and the root resolves up by step. Motion from the diminished fifth into the perfect fifth is often accepted when not between the outer voices. When both tritones are resolved strictly, the resolving tonic chord will have a doubled third.

$$\text{c: vii°7} \quad \text{i} \quad \text{vii°7} \quad \text{i} \quad \text{vii°7} \quad \text{i} \quad \text{vii°7} \quad \text{i}$$

B. For the half-diminished seventh, resolution is the same as for the fully diminished chord except that when the chord third is below the seventh, it cannot resolve down by step because of the parallel perfect fifths that would result. The third must therefore resolve up by step or must be placed above the seventh.

IV. Resolving tendencies are not affected by inversion.

Analysis

Analyze the examples in Unit 14 of *Music for Analysis*. Refer to the Checklist for Analysis (Part V, Unit 21). Bring further examples from the literature into class.

Visit the TMM website eWorkbook exercises, online tutorials, and musical examples with audio for this unit are available at the *Techniques and Materials of Music* website, **TMMTheory.com**.

Exercises

1. Spell vii°7 (fully diminished seventh) in root position and resolve to tonic, using treble clef and signatures, in the following keys: d, D, f, F, e, E, E♭, and e♭.

---

*Note the doubled third.

**Note the doubled root

2. Resolve the leading-tone seventh chord as indicated, and analyze.

3. Harmonize the following melodies, using leading-tone seventh chords where indicated by an asterisk:

a.

b.

c.

d.

4. Realize the following figured basses, using various textures and instrumental combinations. Work for a musical soprano line and smooth voice leading.

a.

b.

c.

d.

5. Complete the following, using the given texture. Analyze completely.

6. Complete the following in the given contrapuntal textures:

a.

b.

(unfigured)

7. The following patterns may be used for composition or improvisation:

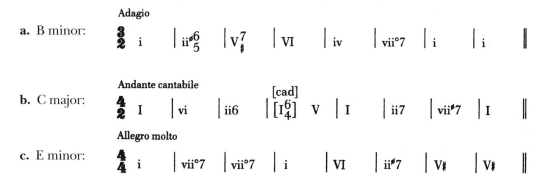

a. B minor:

Adagio

$\frac{3}{2}$ i | ii$^{\sharp 6}_{5}$ | V$^{7}_{\sharp}$ | VI | iv | vii°7 | i | i ‖

b. C major:

Andante cantabile

$\frac{4}{2}$ I | vi | ii6 | [cad] [I$^{6}_{4}$] V | I | ii7 | vii$^{\sharp}$7 | I ‖

c. E minor:

Allegro molto

$\frac{4}{4}$ i | vii°7 | vii°7 | i | VI | ii$^{\sharp}$7 | V$^{\sharp}$ | V$^{\sharp}$ ‖

8. Compose a short work for piano or a group of instruments using a texture and pattern suggested by the instructor and employing leading-tone seventh chords where appropriate. Use the following formal outline:

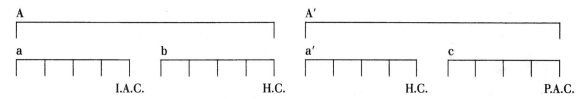

a (8 mm.) $^{H.C.}$ b (8 mm.) $^{I.A.C.}$ b′ (8 mm.) $^{P.A.C.}$

9. Compose a double period for an instrumental combination available in class, employing the period, phrase, and cadence structure outlined here.

A   A′

a   b   a′   c

I.A.C.   H.C.   H.C.   P.A.C.

19 Other Diatonic Seventh Chords

I. A seventh chord may be built on any scale-degree. Of the chords above, the IV7 and vi7 are the most common.

II. The functions of the chords are unaffected by the addition of the seventh.

III. The basic resolution is analogous to the ii7 and V7, with the chord seventh resolving stepwise downward. All diatonic seventh chords occur together most frequently in sequence, going around the circle of fifths. Note that the seventh always resolves regularly and that every other chord is incomplete. All chords will appear complete in thicker textures and in passages in which inversions are used.

IV. A note that appears to be a chord seventh can often be analyzed as a simple nonharmonic tone.

Analysis

Analyze the examples in Unit 15 of *Music for Analysis*. Refer to the Checklist for Analysis (Part V, Unit 21).

eWorkbook exercises, online tutorials, and musical examples with audio for this unit are available at the *Techniques and Materials of Music* website, **TMMTheory.com**.

Exercises

1. Realize the following figured basses.

A step-by-step demonstration of the procedure for realizing a figured bass can be found on the *Techniques and Materials of Music* website, **TMMTheory.com**. A model can also be found in Part V, Unit 10.

a.

b.

c.

2. Harmonize the following melodies, using seventh chords where indicated by the asterisk. These exercises may be done in a two- or three-voice contrapuntal texture.

A step-by-step demonstration of the procedure for harmonizing a melody can be found on the *Techniques and Materials of Music* website, **TMMTheory.com**. A model can also be found in Part V, Unit 11.

a.

b.

c.

d.

3. Use the following bass as the basis for sequential elaboration. This exercise may be done in a two-, three-, or four-voice contrapuntal texture.

4. Compose a four-phrase piece with the form a a′ b b′ for instruments available in class. Keep in mind the possibilities of sequence, phrase extension, cadence structure, and so forth. Employ the complete harmonic vocabulary studied to date. Refer to the Composition Checklist (Part V, Unit 22) and Part V, Unit 23, on instrumental ranges and transpositions.

5. The following patterns may be used for composition or improvisation.

A step-by-step demonstration of the procedure for expansion and elaboration of chord formats can be found on the *Techniques and Materials of Music* website, **TMMTheory.com**. A model can also be found in Part V, Unit 12.

a. F minor:

b. D major:

Allegro

$\frac{3}{4}$ I | IV$^6_5$ | vii$^{\varnothing 4}_2$ | iii$^6_5$ | vi$^4_2$ | ii$^6_5$ | V7 | I ‖

PART

3

Chromatic Materials

Secondary (Applied, Borrowed) Dominants

1

I. *Altered chords* are chords having one or more notes that are not in the diatonic scale of the key of a given passage. (The raised forms of the sixth and seventh scale-degrees in minor are considered diatonic.) The most common type of altered chord in tonal music is the *secondary (applied* or *borrowed) dominant.*

    A. The following are examples of altered chords:

C major

    B. The following are examples of diatonic chords:

C minor

II. Just as the tonic chord is often preceded by its dominant function chords, any major or minor diatonic triad may be preceded by one of its own dominants. For example, the A dominant seventh chord in the following example, found in the key of C major, would be considered altered by virtue of the C♯. It is V7 in the key of D minor. Because the D-minor triad functions as ii in C major, we analyze the altered chord as a *secondary dominant*—V7/ii (read "V7 of ii"). This altered chord could also have other functions in other keys, as follows:

III. A secondary dominant chord usually resolves to its expected chord of resolution using the normal doubling and voice-leading procedures of diatonic dominants. It may also resolve deceptively, as in the last example that follows:

C: $V^7_\#/V$ V $vii^{\circ}{}_b{}^7/V$ V V^6_5/V cad.
$[I^6_4]$ $V^7_\#/vi$ IV
(or V7/vi VI/vi)

IV. Any chord with dominant *quality* (M, Mm7, d, dd7, dm7, or dominant ninth) may function as a secondary dominant. The half-diminished seventh normally resolves to major triads, never to minor triads. The following are the possible chords "of V" in the key of G:

G: $V\#/V$ $V^7_\#/V$ vii°/V $vii^{\#}{}^7/V$ $vii^{\circ}{}_b{}^7/V$ $V^9_\#/V$

V. A secondary dominant chord may substitute for any diatonic chord with the same function. For instance, vi (which usually resolves to ii or IV) may be replaced by a secondary dominant of ii or IV; ii or IV may be replaced by a secondary dominant of V.

C: IV   ii6   V   IV   V6/V   V

VI. A secondary dominant may progress to another secondary dominant, typically as part of the circle of fifths. For instance, the progression V7/ii–ii may be replaced by V7/ii–V7/V because the latter chord can be used to replace ii. Furthermore, secondary dominants of any quality may be freely interchanged, as in example B that follows:

A.   B.

C: iii7   vi7   ii7   V7 $V^7_\#/vi$ $V^7_\#/ii$ $V^7_\#/V$ V7   vii°7/vi $V\#/ii$ V^6_5/V V

diatonic sequence   chromatic sequence

---

*Note doubled third.

VII. Common altered scale-degree formulas follow. These may be useful for determining the harmonic implication of any chromatic note that is clearly a chord tone.

A. For raised scale-degrees, note that the raised note is usually the third of a V (or V7) sound or the root of a vii°7 (or vii°7) sound.

B. For lowered scale-degrees, note that the lowered note is usually the seventh of either a V7 or vii°7 sound.

VIII. Secondary dominants are sometimes preceded by a dominant preparation, as follows:

Analysis

Analyze the examples in Unit 17 of *Music for Analysis*. Consider the following:

1. Where does chromaticism occur?

2. Is the chromaticism essential or embellishing?

3. If it is essential, what harmonic function does it express?

4. Where do the altered chords occur in the phrase?

 eWorkbook exercises, online tutorials, and musical examples with audio for this unit are available at the *Techniques and Materials of Music* website, **TMMTheory.com**.

Visit the
TMM website

Exercises

1. Spell the following chords in G major and B♭ major, in root position; use treble clef and key signatures: V7/V, vii°/V, vii°7/V, vii°7/ii, V/vi, V7/iii, and V7/IV.

2. Spell the following chords in E minor and D minor, in root position; use bass clef and key signatures: V/V, V7/iv, V7/VI, vii°7/V, V7/III, and vii°7/III.

3. Explain what functions a dominant seventh chord built on A would have in the following keys: G, g, F, D, C, and B♭. List keys and analyze functions in roman numerals.

4. Analyze the function of an F♯ fully diminished seventh chord in the following keys: G, g, F, E♭, D, C, c, and B♭.

5. Analyze the given chords and resolve normally.

F: F: F: F:

6. Analyze the given chords and resolve as indicated.

G: I$^6_4$ G: I$^6_4$ G: IV   G: ii6
                                                            (deceptive   (deceptive
                                                            resolution)   resolution)

7. Work out this unfigured bass twice: first as a diatonic sequence of triads and seventh chords, then as a series of secondary dominants.

8. Harmonize in four voices using secondary dominants. Analyze completely, including figured bass symbols.

9. Unfigured bass. Harmonize in four voices, using secondary dominants. Analyze completely.

10. Harmonize the following melodies, using secondary dominants in the appropriate places. Analyze completely.

A step-by-step demonstration of the procedure for harmonizing a melody can be found on the *Techniques and Materials of Music* website, **TMMTheory.com**. A model can also be found in Part V, Unit 11 .

e.

f.

g.

11. Work out the following figured and unfigured basses, using textures and instrumentation suggested by the instructor. Strive for a musical melody and a consistent sense of motion. Analyze completely. Refer to Part V, Unit 9, for information on accidentals in figured bass.

A step-by-step demonstration of the procedure for realizing a figured bass can be found on the *Techniques and Materials of Music* website, **TMMTheory.com**. A model can also be found in Part V, Unit 10.

a.

b.

c.

d.

e.

f.

g.

12. Add a contrapuntal bass voice to the following melody. Refer to Part V, Unit 19, on counterpoint.

Vivo

13. Compose a passacaglia on the following bass. Refer to Part V, Units 19 and 20, on counterpoint and contrapuntal forms.

14. The following patterns may be used for composition or improvisation:

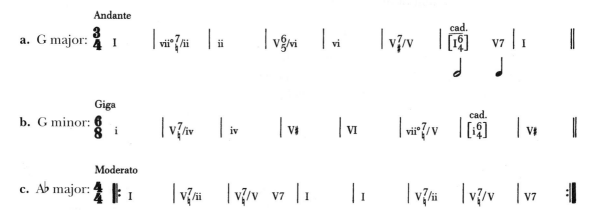

15. Compose a parallel double period for instruments available in class, using secondary dominants where appropriate and based on the following pattern:

a (4 mm.) ⌐H.C.⌐ b (4 mm.) ⌐I.A.C.⌐ a (4 mm.) ⌐H.C.⌐ b' (4 mm.) ⌐P.A.C.⌐

2 Modulation

I. *Modulation* is the process of moving from one tonal center to another, resulting in the clear establishment of the new tonal center. Modulation usually involves three stages: establishment of the first key, the modulatory device, and establishment of the second key.

II. Modulation within the phrase.

   A. Common chord modulation.

   1. The following is a checklist for locating the common (pivot) chord in *common-chord modulation*.

      a. The common chord is *diatonic* in both keys.

      b. The common chord is usually ii or IV in the new key.

      c. The common chord is usually placed immediately before the first dominant function chord, or I$^6_4$, in the new key.

      d. The new key is often indicated by a cadential I$^6_4$ chord.

      e. The new key is usually tonicized by an authentic cadence shortly after the modulation.

      f. All music before the common chord will be functional in the first key; all music from the common chord to the cadence will be functional in the new key.

155

B. Direct modulation. Where direct chromaticism or cross relation occurs at the point of modulation, a *direct (chromatic) modulation* is to be analyzed.

F: I   g: V♯   i

C. Sequential modulation. A sequence passing through a series of secondary dominants may obscure the initial tonality. At any point the sequence may be broken and the new key tonicized by a cadential progression. Refer to the Durante example in Part V, Unit 16.

III. Modulation between phrases. In *phrase modulation,* modulations occur between phrases; that is, a new phrase or section may simply begin in a new key. Even when a potential common chord may be present, such a modulation is analyzed as being of the phrase type. In many small forms, phrase remodulations to the tonic key often occur at the beginning of the second section, as in the example in II—A.

IV. For other means of modulation, see Part III, Unit 6.

V. In analysis, the place where the second key begins is shown in the usual way, with key name and colon, as in II—B. If the modulation is by phrase or is chromatic, a brief note to that effect may be written at that point in the music. If there is a common chord, it is shown with a bracket, as follows:

⎡ first key: ⎡ G:
⎣ second key: such as   ⎣ e:

VI. Most modulations are to closely related keys. *Closely related keys* have key signatures that differ by no more than one accidental. The following chart shows the keys considered most closely related to a given main key:

relative   relative   relative   a   d   g   ⎛ iii   vi   ii
  | | | such as | | | ⎜ | | |
dominant — *main key* — subdominant   C — F — B♭   ⎝ V — I — IV ⎠

                                                 E♭   A♭   D♭
                                and | | |
                                                  c — f — b♭

It is possible to modulate to keys other than those that are closely related by means of the devices discussed above.

Analysis

Look at the examples in Unit 18 of *Music for Analysis*. This unit contains a number of examples that employ binary and ternary formal processes. Consider the following questions, and refer to Part V, Units 13, 15, and 20, on cadence and phrase structure, the motive, and form. Prepare a simple graph of the form, as suggested in Part V, Unit 20, and label (name) the form.

1. Where do cadences occur? Of what types and in what keys are they?

2. How many phrases are there? Is there a periodic relationship?

3. How is the first key established?

4. Where do modulations occur? How are they effected?

5. Are the sections motivically or thematically related?

6. Is material restated, varied, or developed?

 eWorkbook exercises, online tutorials, and musical examples with audio for this unit are available at the *Techniques and Materials of Music* website, **TMMTheory.com**.

Visit the
TMM website

Exercises

1. Analyze the function of an F-major triad in the following keys: F, f, C, d, E♭, a, D♭, b♭, A♭, and B♭. Which are diatonic?

2. Name the keys in which an F-minor triad could have the following functions: i, ii, iii, iv, and vi.

3. Name four diatonic triads that could be used as common chords to modulate between G major and D major, and specify their function in both keys.

4. Apply the preceding question to modulations between the following pairs of keys: g-d, A♭-c, and D-b.

5. Harmonize the following modulating melodies. Work for a musical bass line and good counterpoint between the outer voices. Analyze completely.

A step-by-step demonstration of the procedure for harmonizing a melody can be found on the *Techniques and Materials of Music* website, **TMMTheory.com**. A model can also be found in Part V, Unit 11.

a.

Allegro

b.

Andante cantabile

c.

Moderato

d.

Comodo

e.

Allegro

f.

Fliesend

g.

Ländler

h.

Gigue

i.

Andantino

6. Work out the following basses, both figured and unfigured, using textures and instrumentation as suggested by the instructor. Work for effective melody lines.

A step-by-step demonstration of the procedure for realizing a figured bass can be found on the *Techniques and Materials of Music* website, **TMMTheory.com**. A model can also be found in Part V, Unit 10.

a.

b.

c.

d.

e.

f.

g.

7. Look at several examples of two- or three-voice nonimitative counterpoint in *Music for Analysis*. An index of contrapuntal examples will be found in Appendix 5. Then, complete the following examples in a two- or three-voice contrapuntal texture.

a.

b.

8. The following patterns may be used for composition and improvisation in a variety of textures, including two- and three-voice counterpoint:

d. E minor: (Lamentoso)

e. E major: (Allegro)

f. A♭ major: (Moderato)

9. Construct original harmonic frameworks of eight to sixteen measures, in roman numerals, modulating between the following pairs of keys: G–e, f–A♭, B♭–c, and D–A. Write melodies based on these frameworks, and harmonize the melodies, using appropriate textures.

10. Analyze simple examples of nonimitative counterpoint as suggested by the instructor. Compose a simple two-voice Baroque binary suite movement, as follows:

Modulate to the dominant key in the first half and back to the tonic in the second. Refer to Part V, Unit 19, on counterpoint.

3 Linear (Embellishing) Diminished Seventh Chords

I. Simultaneous nonharmonic tones frequently form diminished seventh chords. Like other linear chords, these *linear (embellishing) diminished seventh chords* are analyzed in brackets. Because these chords occur with various enharmonic spellings, they are best analyzed simply by chord quality (dd7) along with the category of nonharmonic tone use.

II. Neighboring (auxiliary) chords.

A. Embellished major triads.

    1. The root remains stationary.

    2. The third moves to the raised lower neighbor.

    3. The fifth moves to the upper neighbor and/or to the raised lower neighbor.

B. Minor triads rarely have neighboring chords. When they do, both the root and third remain stationary, and the fifth moves up a *major* second and/or down a minor second.

C. For dominant seventh chords the voice leading is as in the major triad, with the seventh also moving to its lower neighbor.

D. When an inverted triad is embellished, the stationary root will be in one of the upper voices.

III. Passing chords. When two voices move in parallel sixths or tenths, passing chords may result. Note that in the first example, the first of the passing chords is diatonic, and the second, chromatic.

IV. Linear diminished seventh chords may result from combinations of other kinds of nonharmonic tones.

V. Consecutive stepwise diminished seventh chords may be analyzed either as a series of secondary dominants or as a series of passing chords. Because of spelling discrepancies, however, the latter is generally preferable.

---

*This chord may also be analyzed as a misspelled vii°7/V chord.

	D:	I	vii°7/ii	vii°7/V	vii°7/vi	vii°7/IV	vii°7/V	vii°$^4_3$	I6
or	D:	I	[passing chords _____]					vii°$^4_3$	I6

Analysis

Analyze the examples in Unit 20 of *Music for Analysis*. In addition to matters discussed thus far, consider the following:

1. Where does the chromaticism occur?

2. Is the chromaticism embellishing or essential?

3. If it is embellishing, are linear chords formed?

4. What is the quality of the linear chords?

5. What is their melodic relationship to the chords they embellish?

eWorkbook exercises, online tutorials, and musical examples with audio for this unit are available at the *Techniques and Materials of Music* website, **TMMTheory.com**.

Visit the
TMM website

Exercises

1. Embellish the given chords with neighboring diminished seventh chords where indicated by an asterisk. Analyze completely.

| | G: | V7 | V7 | B♭: | I6 | I6 | a: | i | i | A♭: | I | I |

2. Add passing chords of any appropriate type where indicated by an asterisk.

3. Where indicated by asterisks, interpolate consecutive stepwise diminished seventh chords between the two chords given. Spelling will be dictated by line. Analyze completely.

4. Embellish the given chords with linear diminished seventh chords where indicated by asterisks.

5. Complete the following for two solo instruments with accompaniment. Use linear diminished seventh chords where appropriate. Edit fully, including phrasing, articulations, and dynamics.

6. Harmonize the following melody in the indicated texture, using linear diminished seventh chords where indicated by an asterisk:

"Les Postludes . . ."

7. Compose an original piece for piano or instruments in a small form. Employ a thick texture containing multiple doublings. Refer to Part V, Units 17, 20, and 22, on texture, form, and composition.

8. The following patterns may be used for composition or improvisation. Add linear diminished seventh chords where appropriate.

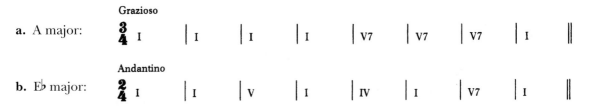

9. Compose a double period for an instrumental combination available in class, employing the period, phrase, and cadence structure outlined here. (Refer to Part V, Unit 23, for information on instrumental ranges and transpositions.)

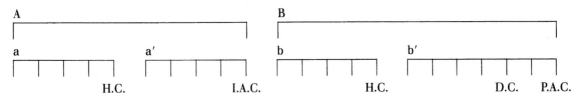

4 The Neapolitan Triad

I. The *Neapolitan triad* is a major triad built on the lowered second scale-degree. Note that in the major mode two alterations are required, and in the minor mode, only one. Because the chord frequently occurs in first inversion, it is often spoken of as a *Neapolitan sixth chord* (analyzed N6).

II. The chord has the same function as a diatonic ii chord and most often occurs preceding a cadence. The third is most commonly doubled, and the root and fifth tend to move down to tones of V or V7. The doubled third may remain stationary and become the seventh of V7.

III. Other uses of the N6 chord follow:

C: N6   vii°7/V   V   d: iv6   III6   N6   i6   vii°6

e: i6   [n.c. N6]   i6   vii°⅚   V⁷♯   i

IV. The N or N6 chord may be used for modulation to both closely and distantly related keys.

  A. The N chord in key 1 becomes any diatonic major triad in key 2.

  B. Any diatonic major triad in key 1 becomes the N chord in key 2.

D: N =   E♭:I   A♭:V   E♭:I   A♭:V   = D: N
           B♭:IV   g:VI   B♭:IV   g:VI

f: i   V⁷♮   i   VI   [f:VI6 / c:N6]   V⁷♮   i

c: i   vii°⅚   i6   [c: N♭6 / A♭:IV♭6]   V♭⁶₅   I

Analysis

Analyze the examples in Unit 21 of *Music for Analysis.* Refer to the Checklist for Analysis in Part V, Unit 21.

↗

Visit the
TMM website
eWorkbook exercises, online tutorials, and musical examples with audio for this unit are available at the *Techniques and Materials of Music* website, **TMMTheory.com.**

Exercises

1. Spell the Neapolitan triad in root position in the following keys:

e: G: F: A♭   c: E: F♯:

2. Write the following progressions in four voices; show the resolution of $\flat\hat{2}$. Employ contrary motion in the outer voices.

d: N♭6   V♯   N♭6   V$^4_2$ N♭6   i$^6_4$

D: N♭6_♭3   V   N♭6_♭3   I$^6_4$ N♭6_♭3   V$^4_2$ N♭6_♭3   I6

3. Realize the following figured basses:

a.

♯4
3   6   7
♯   ♭6   6
4   7
♯

b.

c.

4. Harmonize the following melodies, using Neapolitan triads where appropriate. Analyze completely.

a.

Andante

b.

Moderato

c.

Allegro

5. The following excerpt is from a Vivaldi concerto for violin and organ. Complete the realization of the figured bass in the indicated texture. Then, using the same bass line and chords as a basis, write an original violin line, using Vivaldi as a model. Analyze all work completely.

Vivaldi

Grave

Violin

Organ

6. The following patterns may be used for composition or improvisation:

7. Compose a phrase group for an instrumental combination available in class, employing the cadence structure outlined here.

5 Augmented Sixth Chords

Minor mode:

c:	Italian (It.)	German (Ger.)	French (Fr.)
diatonic basis:	iv	iv7	ii⁴7
scale-degrees:	♯4, 6, 1	♯4, 6, 1, 3	2, ♯4, 6, 1

Major mode:

C:	It.	Ger.	Fr.	Enharmonic (En.) Ger.
scale-degrees:	♯4, ♭6, 1	♯4, ♭6, 1, ♭3	2, ♯4, ♭6, 1	♯2, ♯4, ♭6, 1

These chords are given above simply for spelling; in a musical context they are most often found as shown in III, below, and subsequent examples.

I. *Augmented sixth chords* are chords containing the interval of the augmented sixth (A6). The four augmented sixth chords are all altered chords. They most often function as dominant preparations, especially at cadential points, and can be used to replace IV, ii, or secondary dominants of V. The distinctions among the augmented sixth chords are not always clear in context.

II. Each augmented sixth chord contains the tonic note and the raised fourth and lowered sixth scale-degrees (both surrounding and tending toward the dominant note). In both modes an accidental is required to raise the fourth scale-degree; in the major mode an accidental also is needed to lower the sixth scale-degree. Note further that the German chord requires a lowered third scale-degree in major, and the Enharmonic German, a raised second scale-degree.

III. The augmented sixth chords are shown in the following example in their most common position, with the sixth scale-degree in the bass. Note the three common tones between all four chords and the augmented sixth interval between the bass and tenor voices, which gives rise to the chord's name. Note the doubled tonic scale-degree (the fifth of the chord) in the Italian chord. The Enharmonic German chord is sometimes called the *chord of the doubly augmented fourth* (from A flat to D sharp in this example). It is used to facilitate resolution to a cadential tonic six-four chord.

173

IV. Augmented sixth chords are similar to, and function like, secondary dominants of V. Note the doubled tonic scale-degree in the Italian chord. The altered notes in these chords are tendency tones and should not be doubled.

V. The augmented sixth chords usually resolve to V, V7, or I$^6_4$. The A6 resolves outward by step to a P8 or P15, and the other tones usually resolve by step. Composers sometimes accept the parallel fifths arising when the German chord resolves to V, but see paragraph VI, below.

Inversions do not affect resolving tendencies.

VI. To avoid the parallel fifths resulting from the resolution of the German sixth to V, composers often change the German chord to an Italian or French chord before its resolution. Note the scale-degree changes that result in the alteration of one augmented sixth into another.

When the augmented sixth chords resolve to V7 rather than V, the raised fourth scale-degree often resolves downward (rather than upward, as usual) by a half step to form the seventh of the V7.

VII. Other uses of augmented sixth chords.

   A. Augmented sixth chords may be used as dominant function chords resolving to the tonic triad. In this case they are best analyzed as V7 with a lowered chord fifth (V7♭5) or as vii°7 with a lowered chord third (vii°♭3). These most often occur with the second scale-degree in the bass (causing a V$^4_3$ or vii°$^6_5$ Position).

   B. Augmented sixth chords may be used as secondary dominant preparation chords, leading to secondary dominants.

   C. Augmented sixth chords may be used as linear chords, treated as neighbors or appoggiaturas. Compare these chords to the linear diminished seventh chords illustrated in Part III, Unit 3.

   Note in the following examples that two voices surround the fifth of the chord being ornamented, and resolve by half step into that note.

---

*As in the resolution of Ger. $^6_5$–V, composers often accept these parallel fifths.

C: I6   [En. Ger. n.c.]   I6   V   [En. Ger. n.c.]   V

D. Augmented sixth chords may be used as modulatory devices. See Part III, Unit 6.

Analysis

Analyze the examples in Units 22 to 24 of *Music for Analysis*. Be aware, as always, of such elements as motive, line, rhythmic structure, texture, and formal processes. In addition, consider the following:

1. Does the harmonic vocabulary contain augmented sixth chords?

2. Which types are they?

3. Where are they placed in the phrase?

4. How are they related to the chords immediately preceding and following them?

eWorkbook exercises, online tutorials, and musical examples with audio for this unit are available at the *Techniques and Materials of Music* website, **TMMTheory.com**.

Visit the
TMM website

Exercises

1. Analyze the given augmented sixth chords and resolve as indicated.

D: [I⁶₄]   V   d: [i⁶₄]   V♯

2. Analyze and resolve the following chords:

3. Spell and resolve the augmented sixth chords as indicated. Show the resolution of the augmented sixth and show any common tones.

4. Spell and resolve the indicated chords. Show the resolution of all tendency tones, and show any common tones.

5. Harmonize the following melodies and realize the figured and unfigured basses, using augmented sixth chords as indicated by asterisks. Work for strong outer voices and smooth voice leading. Analyze all work completely.

a.

6. Complete the following progressions, employing variant uses of augmented sixth chords as indicated:

7. The following patterns may be used for composition or improvisation using various textures and instruments as suggested by the instructor:

8. Compose a theme and at least three variations for instruments available in class. The theme should be a simple binary form, and the harmonic language should reflect that studied so far. Analyze completely.

6 Modulation by Other Means

The following are devices that may be used to modulate between both closely and distantly related keys.

I. Any fully diminished seventh chord can be heard as belonging to several different keys and may be respelled to resolve in any of those keys; thus this chord is useful in modulation. The enharmonically respelled chords may function as dominants, secondary dominants, or linear chords in either or both keys. Furthermore, any member of a diminished seventh chord may be lowered a minor second to change that chord to a dominant seventh.

A. Modulation to closely related keys.

B. Modulation to distantly related keys.

II. The German augmented sixth chord (and Enharmonic German chord) sounds like a dominant seventh, so it can be approached as one function and left as the other. A respelled German chord may become either V7 or any secondary dominant seventh chord, or any dominant seventh chord may be respelled as a German chord.

A. Ger. $\frac{6}{5}$ becomes V7.

B. V7 becomes Ger. $\frac{6}{5}$.

III. In common-tone modulation, a single note common to two keys may be used as a pivot between those keys. The common tone is most often a member of the tonic triad of one or both keys.

The common note may be enharmonic.

Ab: I   V7   I   I6   E: [I⁶₄]   V♯⁷₅   I⁵₃
                                              cad.   ♯

Analysis

Analyze the examples in Unit 25 of *Music for Analysis.* In addition to matters discussed thus far, consider the following:

1. Where do modulations occur?

2. By what means are they achieved?

3. What keys are involved? What is the intervallic relationship between the tonics?

eWorkbook exercises, online tutorials, and musical examples with audio for this unit are available at the *Techniques and Materials of Music* website, **TMMTheory.com.**

Visit the
TMM website

Exercises

1. Harmonize the following basses and melodies, and analyze:

a.

Eb: V7   D: Ger.⁶₅   [I⁶₄]

b.

g: vii°7 _____ i6   iv6   Bb: vii°7 _____ I

c.

6   6   6   7   6   7   ⌀   6   7   �g
5   5   ♭5   5   4   ♯
               ♯

d.

e.

2. Write modulating pieces of period length as indicated:

Key 1	Key 2	Method of Modulation
G	f♯	Neapolitan chord
e	G	diminished seventh chord
E♭	G	German chord
E	F	Neapolitan chord
D	E♭	German chord
B♭	A	German chord
G	B	common tone
D♭	A	common tone

3. Discuss choral composition; sing and analyze works from the choral literature. Select a brief text, and compose a short choral setting using materials discussed thus far. Modulate at least once, using one of the means discussed in this unit.

4. Compose a nonperiodic phrase-group for piano or instrumental combination; it should contain modulations by any of the devices discussed thus far.

Ninth Chords

$$g: \quad V^9_\sharp \qquad\qquad G: \quad V9 \qquad\qquad V\flat 9$$
$$\text{(Mmm9)} \qquad\qquad \text{(MmM9)} \quad or \quad \text{(Mmm9)}$$

I. A *dominant ninth chord (V9)* is a major triad with a minor seventh and a major or minor ninth. With a major ninth, the chord resolves only to a major triad or other seventh chord.

   A. The V9 chord has dominant function and can be used to replace any other dominant function chord except at a half cadence.

   B. Ninth chords are usually found spaced fairly widely, with the ninth always at least a ninth above the root. All inversions are possible, but the fourth inversion is very rare. Figured-bass symbols for inverted ninth chords are unwieldy and are not used in this text. The chord fifth is often omitted. In resolving to I, the ninth resolves down by step, and the other tones resolve as in V7. The ninth often resolves before the rest of the chord, in which case it may be analyzed as a nonharmonic tone. These chords often occur in thicker textures.

   C. The V7 or V9 chords with raised or lowered chord fifths are found in much late romantic music. For a discussion, refer to Part IV, Unit 4.

II. A *nondominant ninth chord* functions similarly to a nondominant seventh chord and is built over the same scale-degrees. i9, ii9, iii9, iv9, and vi9 are possible. Most nondominant ninths have one of the following qualities: mmM9 or MMM9. Resolution is like that of the dominant ninth, with the chord typically resolving to a seventh chord or another ninth chord.

G: vi9   ii7   ii9   V9   g: iv9   V♯7   vi9   ii♯7

Nondominant or dominant ninth effects may occur over a pedal point, in which case several alternative analyses may be possible.

G: ii   ⎡n.c.⎤   ii   ii   vi/ii *   ii   ii _____
             ⎣ii9⎦

Analysis

Analyze the examples in Unit 26 of *Music for Analysis*, keeping in mind elements previously considered.

eWorkbook exercises, online tutorials, and musical examples with audio for this unit are available at the *Techniques and Materials of Music* website, **TMMTheory.com**.

Exercises

1. Resolve the following V9 chords to tonic in root position:

D: V9   I   V9   I   d: V♯9   i   V♯9   i

*This is read "vi over ii root."

2. Resolve the following nondominant ninth chords as indicated:

F: vi9   ii7   ii9   V9   e: i9   iv7   III9   VI7

3. Resolve the following inverted V9 chords as indicated:

B♭:   V9   I   V♭9   I6   V9   I6   V♭9   I6

4. Work out the following melodies and basses, using ninth chords where indicated. Articulate the bass lines in a typical romantic piano texture, and use a fairly full sonority. Analyze completely.

a.

G: V9/V   V

b.

       9   9   9   9   9 - 8   9 - 8

c.

d: V♯7   9   i   V♯9/iv   iv   V♯9/V   V♯

d.

b: ♮7   9 - 8 9 - 8   9 - 8 - 7   9 - 8
                                           ♯———————————

5. Select one of the following forms: rounded binary, ternary, or theme and variations. Write an instrumental work for resources available in class, or study text-setting and write an extended choral work or solo song with piano or instrumental accompaniment. The harmonic vocabulary should represent the materials and techniques covered thus far. Refer to the Composition Checklist (Part V, Unit 22).

PART 4

Twentieth-Century Materials

Twentieth-Century Techniques: General Comments

The music of the twentieth century is remarkably diverse in its styles and techniques. There is no single common practice in this music, but rather a wide spectrum of materials and treatments. The authors have chosen to deal briefly with many of the most widely used of these materials and techniques in the following units, as an introduction to the much larger subject of twentieth-century music. Please take careful note of the following general points.

I. The specific *details* of traditional part-writing apply less strictly to twentieth-century music, but the underlying *principles* are the same.

  A. *Parallelism* of all types of intervals, including perfect fifths, is common, but the *principles of linear independence* are often the same as in tonal music.

  B. Chords may be built of intervals other than thirds, but the *general considerations of good-sounding spacing* still apply.

  C. Chords may be highly dissonant, but the necessity for *harmonic and textural consistency* still applies. The concepts of consonance and dissonance are not necessarily the same as for older music, nor are they necessarily consistent between given twentieth-century works. *Each work typically establishes its own norms of consonance and dissonance.*

II. Any given piece of twentieth-century music may involve several of the techniques and materials under discussion in the following pages. Few works clearly exemplify only one technique. However, certain techniques and devices tend to be mutually exclusive (for example, modality and serialism).

III. Much twentieth-century music is clearly built around a central tone but lacks the harmonic functions associated with traditional tonality. This music is frequently referred to as *centric*. The use of key signatures is optional and depends on the composer, even with centric music.

IV. Certain techniques or styles of twentieth-century music typically start with only a limited number of pitches (for example, pentatonic or modal music), whereas others regularly use all twelve notes of the chromatic scale. The former tend to be predominantly diatonic, with chromaticism used for variety or increased intensity; the latter tend toward more complex harmonic relationships and a higher dissonance level.

V. *Planing* (pronounced with a long *a*) is a technique involving parallelism of lines or chords. There are two types: chromatic (exact, real) planing, in which the chord structure or harmonic interval is preserved exactly from sound to sound;

and diatonic (tonal) planing, where because of the presence of a particular scale, slightly different chords or intervals in successive sonorities may result. Diatonic planing usually supports a feeling of key and scale, whereas chromatic planing does not.

A. Chromatic planing.

B. Diatonic planing.

VI. According to the *transposition factor*, any collection of notes will contain certain intervals. If any interval, including inversional equivalents (for example, M2 = m7), is missing in the set, the collection may be transposed by that interval to yield an entirely new collection of notes. Other transpositions will yield one or more notes in common with the original collection. Compositional use can be made of these facts in terms of achieving variety while still using a restricted set of intervals.

Basic collection, lacking m2 (= M7) and A4 (= d5)

Transpositions by m2 and A4 (no common notes with basic collection)

2 Chord Symbols and Approaches to Analysis

Note: Octave doublings and spacings are not taken into account in the following analytic systems.

I. Additional systems.

A. Popular music (jazz) lead sheet symbols.

Chord symbols are not standardized, and students are apt to encounter variations of those given above, especially in manuscript arrangements.

Visit the *Techniques and Materials of Music* website at **TMMTheory.com** for musical examples, reference materials, and a quiz on jazz-pop chord symbols.

Visit the
TMM website

B. Because of the complexity of many contemporary chord structures, neither roman numerals nor chord symbols are satisfactory for analysis. For this reason, a number of alternate systems have been devised. These systems have in common the analysis of a group of associated pitches (for instance, a chord, scale, or melodic line) by the quality and number of its constituent intervals. In addition, the Hindemith system seeks to identify a chord root. This root will be the one note that appears as the root of the strongest interval(s) found within the chord.

1. Hanson system.

   Noting the inability of more traditional analytic methods adequately to describe most twentieth-century music, Howard Hanson, in his book *Harmonic Materials of Modern Music* (see Bibliography for the details), invented a simple system of interval labeling, given below. In this system (as in most interval-descriptive systems), octave (registral) placement, octave doubling, spacing, and voicing are not accounted for. Octave equivalence and equal temperament are assumed as givens. All instances in a sonority of the pitch "D" are understood as the "pitch-class D" and are equivalent for analytic purposes. Any collection of pitches (such as a scale, melodic line, or chord) may be analyzed using the Hanson system. Thus, the sonority:

   is reduced for analytic purposes to:

   In this system, the symbols p, m, n, s, d, and t stand for interval classes:

p	=	perfect intervals
m	=	major thirds and minor sixths
n	=	minor thirds and major sixths
s	=	minor sevenths and major seconds
d	=	major sevenths and minor seconds
t	=	tritones

   In the analysis of a sonority, the symbols are always given in order, with superscript numbers showing the number of a given interval class in the given sonority.

   When using any interval-descriptive system, it is useful to know the number of intervals in any set of notes. The formula $n(n-1)/2$ may be used to provide a quick calculation.

In the example given above, there are four pitches, so there will be six intervals $[(4 \times 3)/2 = 6]$. Here are two other examples:

pdt $p^4mn^2s^3$

2. Persichetti system.

Vincent Persichetti, in his book *Twentieth Century Harmony* (see Bibliography for the details), dealt with the matter of describing nonconventional sonorities via interval labeling by devising a graphic system of interval labeling. This system is similar to that of Hanson in that octave placement, octave doubling, spacing, and voicing are not accounted for, and pitch-class equivalency is assumed. Persichetti's system differs from that of Hanson in that intervals are grouped in four categories. *Consonance* includes all perfect intervals plus all thirds, both major and minor, and all sixths, both major and minor. *Mild dissonance* includes major seconds and minor sevenths. *Sharp dissonance* includes minor seconds and major sevenths. *Neutral dissonance* indicates the tritone.

(= consonances (Hanson's p, m, n)
[= mild dissonances (Hanson's s)
< = sharp dissonances (Hanson's d)
⠁ = neutral dissonances (Hanson's t)

3. Hindemith system of root designation.

In his book *The Craft of Musical Composition* (see Bibliography for the details), Paul Hindemith describes a method of root designation for vertical sonorities. This approach is based on the overtone series (see Part V, Unit 2) and is consistent with our understanding of root structure in tertian harmonies. The example below indicates the intervals, left to right, in increasing order of dissonance, from the octave through to the tritone. The root of each interval is indicated. Note that the tritone, ambiguous in character, by its nature has no root.

consonance ⟵——————————————————————————⟶ dissonance

In the following sonorities, the root of each "chord" is determined by its primacy in the structure. The pitch that is supported by the majority of intervals within a "chord," with intervals toward the bottom of the stack predominating, is understood to be its root. Thus, in the first instance,

B♭ is the root of the stack, as it is the root of the lowest interval, the perfect fourth. In the second structure, F is the root of the two lowest intervals, the minor second and the major third, and also the majority of intervals in the stack, and is thus the root of the "chord." In the third "chord," F is the root of the majority of intervals as well as the lowest intervals, the perfect fifth, the minor seventh, and the minor third (tenth).

4. Allen Forte, Joel Lester, and many others have developed a method for analyzing atonal and serial music. *Pitch- and interval-class theory* (related to mathematical set theory) in effect also reduces a complex of notes into its constituent intervals and, much like the Hanson system, enumerates the intervals according to type. In the first example below, the numbers within the brackets indicate that there is one m2 or M7, one P4 or P5, one TT, and no other intervals.

Set 3-5: [0,1,6]   Set 4-14: [0,2,3,7]   Set 5-35: [0,2,4,7,0]
Vector [100011]   Vector [111120]   Vector [032140]

It is beyond the scope of this book to deal with any of these systems in detail. A more detailed discussion may be found in Unit 10 on pages 227–231 and in online resources provided at **TMMTheory.com**. The standard books dealing with these systems are all listed in the Bibliography.

II. In addition to the usual items covered in analysis, with twentieth-century music, the following questions should also be considered:

A. Is the music centric? If so, how is the tonal center established?

B. What scalar material is used?

C. What harmonic materials are used? Is there a sense of harmonic progression? If so, how is it controlled? What is the normative dissonance level? How is it established and controlled?

D. What cadential idioms and devices are employed?

E. What rhythmic and metric devices are used?

III. Suggested reading (see the Bibliography): Hanson, Hindemith, Persichetti, Forte.†

eWorkbook exercises, online tutorials, and musical examples with audio for this unit are available at the *Techniques and Materials of Music* website, **TMMTheory.com**.

Visit the
TMM website

---

†Supplementary readings are suggested at the end of most units in Part IV; these books are listed in the Bibliography. The student will also find that reference to the various anthologies listed there, as well as to such collections as the *Mikro-kosmos* of Bartók, is essential.

3 Rhythmic and Metric Devices

Perhaps the most characteristically original aspect of twentieth-century music is its rhythm. The various devices used are in marked contrast with the metric regularity of common practice music with its functional rhythmic patterns (for example, march or dance) and regular four-bar phrases. Twentieth-century music is often asymmetric; it has complex rhythmic/metric patterns and occasionally gives the effect of unpredictability or great freedom. In certain styles meters are simply omitted; this music is termed *ametrical*.

I. *Irregular meters* are those whose upper numbers are not divisible by 2 or 3 (for example, 5, 7, 11, and 13). The accents fall in alternate two- and three-beat groups.

A. Irregular meters may be simple or compound: $\frac{5}{4}$ or $\frac{15}{8}$. *Composite meters* such as $\frac{5}{8}$ and $\frac{7}{8}$ are irregular meters that represent alternate simple and compound beats, with the value of the eighth note remaining constant. The patterns of twos and threes may remain the same throughout or vary from measure to measure.

B. An even number of notes can also be organized in composite patterns.

II. In *changing (mixed) meters*, the variables are the number of different meters involved, the number of beats in each meter, and the basic note values of each meter. When two meters having the same unit of beat alternate, the effect is of a composite meter.

A. Meters having different lower numbers may alternate. In such cases, one common note value will generally remain constant, and the effect will again be that of a composite meter.

B. Larger patterns of recurring meters are also possible. Meters employing varying numbers and units of beats may be freely intermixed.

C. Effects similar to those previously illustrated may be achieved by using accent marks to displace the normal metric accents.

III. Jazz syncopation typically involves a displacement within a regular meter by use of the tie into the strong beat.

IV. Complex rhythmic effects can be achieved by juxtaposing varying rhythmic divisions but keeping a common measure *(polyrhythms).*

This effect can also be achieved by juxtaposing different metric patterns, keeping a common note value *(polymeters).*

Isorhythmic effects involve recurring rhythmic patterns (rhythmic ostinatos) that do not necessarily coincide with pitch patterns.

V. Ametrical rhythmic effects are best notated without a meter signature and without bar lines.

VI. Suggestions for class discussions.

    A. Bring examples from the literature into class.

        B. Analyze examples that use many changes of meter.

           1. Is there an overall pattern of repetition?

           2. What relationship exists between the metric patterns and the phrase structure?

           3. What determines the choice of a particular meter?

        C. Suggested reading (see the Bibliography): Dallin, Persichetti, DeLone.

eWorkbook exercises, online tutorials, and musical examples with audio for this unit are available at the *Techniques and Materials of Music* website, **TMMTheory.com**.

Visit the
TMM website

Exercises

1. Write brief excerpts for unpitched percussion instruments characterized as follows:

    a. In an irregular (composite) meter

    b. Using extensive meter changes

    c. Using accent marks to displace the normal metric accent

2. Write a piece for percussion ensemble, employing polyrhythms and polymeters.

4 Tertian Harmony

I. Traditional *tertian chords* (chords built of thirds) persisted into the twentieth century.

    A. Composers use triads of all qualities, including *"indeterminate" triads* (in a tertian context, chords with omitted thirds):

        C   Cm   C+   F♯°   C ind

    B. "Tall" chords are built by superimposing (stacking) major and minor thirds. The following types of chords are possible.

        1. Traditional sevenths and ninths, either dominant or nondominant.

      Dm9   Fmaj9   F9   Dm9-5   Em9+7

        2. "Taller" chords constructed by adding thirds beyond the ninth to form dominant or nondominant elevenths or thirteenths.

      Dm9(+11) Dm13(+11) D9(+11) D13(+11)

These chords are found most often in root position, with the wider spacings toward the bottom. The uppermost members of the chord (ninth, eleventh, thirteenth, etc.) typically occur in the highest voices. The fifth, and occasionally the third, may be omitted. Very close spacing of these chords, which emphasizes seconds, yields a clusterlike effect. (See Part IV, Unit 8.)

    Gm11   D♭13

    Gm9   Am7/D   cluster

C. Some of the most common chords are altered dominants. These include ninths and elevenths with raised and/or lowered fifths, and V7 or V9 with both major and minor thirds (often spelled as a raised ninth).

G7 − 5   G9 + 5   G7 + 9

D. *Superposed chords* and *suspensive chords* are similar to tall chords or added note chords with omitted tones; compare them to polychords.

$\frac{C}{D}$ $\frac{Dm7}{G}$ $\frac{Em9}{A}$ $\frac{E}{A}$ Dm7(susp. 4)   E(susp.)

E. *Added note chords* are most frequently those with an M2 (or M9) or an M6 above the root of a major or minor triad.

G6   G9   G6(add 9)

The presence of the seventh in an ádded note chord may result in the sound of a tall chord.

G^{13}_{9}

II. Chord relationships.

    A. In "functional" root relationships, triads and tall chords may progress quasi-functionally, with root relationships of a fourth and fifth. This is particularly true of altered dominants, which tend to progress around the circle of fifths. Tall chords are now found with "tonic" function. Sevenths and ninths are no longer necessarily considered linear dissonances requiring resolution.

    B. In "nonfunctional" root relationships, chords may be associated without reference to traditional tonality. Roots typically move by seconds and thirds. Abrupt modulations and juxtapositions of remote key areas are often the result.

| A | Fm | D | | E | Dm6 | E | Gm |

III. Suggestions for class discussion.

    A. Analyze the examples in Unit 30 of *Music for Analysis*. Students may bring additional examples from the literature into class.

    B. Suggested reading (see the Bibliography): Dallin, Persichetti, Ulehla.

visit the TMM website

eWorkbook exercises, online tutorials, and musical examples with audio for this unit are available at the *Techniques and Materials of Music* website, **TMMTheory.com**.

Exercises

    1. Identify the following chords, using standard chord symbols written above the treble staff. Use the system of chord description found in Part IV, Unit 2, and in this Unit.

    2. Using the great staff, write the designated chords, using voicings similar to the chords in EXERCISE 1. Voice the left hand with two to three notes, with wide spacing in the lowest voices; voice the right hand with four to five notes in close spacing. All chords should be in root position.

    E♭ maj.9, A6, Dm9/G, F9(♯11), Gm(maj.7), Dm9, Gmaj.11, A♭9, F♯m7/B, F13

3. Complete the harmonization of the melody as directed. Analyze all chords. See ID and IIA and IIB in this Unit for examples.

4. Complete the realization of the given bass line as directed. Analyze all chords.

5. Analyze the harmonic structures of the given material, and then complete, using the same vocabulary.

a.

b.

c.

6. Harmonize the following melody, using only triads and seventh chords. Experiment with planing and remote root relationships. Try to avoid common practice clichés.

7. Study the Shostakovich *Prelude, op. 34, no. 24* (#381 in *Music for Analysis*). Then, add an accompaniment to the following in a similar rapidly shifting ("wrong note") style, with abrupt or startling tonal or modal shifts. An additional example of this technique is the Gavotte from the Prokofiev *Classical Symphony* (#463 in *Music for Analysis*).

8. Compose a brief work for piano, employing dominant and nondominant tall chords in an essentially nonfunctional context. Include some examples of chromatic planing.

9. Compose a passage for string quintet based on the following progression: I–V7/vi–V9/ii–V9/V–V9–vi9–ii9–V9–I. Alter several of the chords as discussed in paragraph II.

10. Write a brief passage in a "cocktail piano" idiom employing planed nondominant tall chords and altered dominant elevenths and thirteenths.

11. The following pattern may be used for composition or improvisation in a jazz or popular idiom:

F major: **Bright**
¢ Fmaj7 | Fmaj7 | Fm7 | B♭9 | E♭maj7 |

| E♭maj7 | E♭m7 | A♭9 | D♭maj7 | B♭m B♭m6 |

| F6/C bass | D7-9 | Dm7/G bass | G♭$^{\sharp 11}_{9}$ | Fmaj7 | Fmaj7 ‖

5 The Diatonic (Church) Modes

I. The *diatonic (church) modes (mode* is the same as *scale)* follow in the standard terminology in their un-transposed (white note) forms. The Ionian mode is not shown because it is the equivalent of the major scale. The distinguishing intervals of each mode are bracketed.

II. The modes are defined by tonic (final), scale-degree relationships, and certain typical melodic cadence formulas.

    A. The Dorian, Phrygian, and Aeolian are often regarded as minor modes. Aeolian has the same structure of interval relationships as natural minor. Dorian is similar to natural minor with a raised sixth scale-degree. Phrygian is similar to natural minor with a lowered second scale-degree. The tonic triads of these modes are minor.

    B. The Lydian and Mixolydian are often regarded as major modes. Lydian is similar to major with a raised fourth scale-degree. Mixolydian is similar to major with a lowered seventh scale-degree. The tonic triads of these modes are major.

    C. The Locrian has a diminished tonic triad and is used less than the other modes.

    D. Some typical cadence formulas follow:

III. Characteristic treatment.

    A. Accidentals should be used sparingly so as not to obscure the sense of mode. The last chord of a piece in a minor mode is often major or omits the third of the tonic triad. The tonic must be clearly defined by means of repetition, return, and emphasis in line and cadences. The sense of modality is often brought out by emphasis on a strongly characteristic scale-degree.

B. It is possible to change modes over a single tonic or to transpose a mode to a new tonic for variety. Modes may be mixed freely within a given passage (the mixture of Dorian and Aeolian is typical). Two or more modes may be used simultaneously for an effect of polymodality. (See Part IV, Unit 9, for a discussion of polytonality.)

IV. Modes may be transposed to another tonic. One method for determining the key signature for a transposed mode follows.

A. Determine the relationship of the tonic of the untransposed mode to C.

B. Determine the note that has the same relationship to the tonic of the transposed mode.

C. Determine the major key signature for that note.

Example: Find the key signature of Phrygian mode with F♯ as the tonic.

V. *Scale and chord.* Modal music tends toward tertian harmony, often with root progressions that emphasize the characteristic modal degrees. Planing is typical. Pandiatonic techniques can be effective (see Unit 6). Quartal harmony can also be used in modal contexts (see Unit 8).

VI. Suggestions for class discussion.

A. Analyze the examples in Unit 31 of *Music for Analysis.* Students may bring additional examples from the literature into class.

B. Carefully analyze and compare all the modes in terms of interval relationships, both (1) between the tonic and other scale-degrees above it, and (2) between adjacent scale-degrees.

C. Practice transposing the modes onto various finals, both with and without key signatures (Dorian on G, Lydian on B♭, and so forth).

D. Suggested reading (see the Bibliography): Dallin, Hindemith, Persichetti, Ulehla.

eWorkbook exercises, online tutorials, and musical examples with audio for this unit are available at the *Techniques and Materials of Music* website, **TMMTheory.com**.

Visit the
TMM website

Exercises

1. Identify the following transposed modes.

2. Using the Grand Staff, write the indicated modes in both treble and bass clef: F♯ Aeolian, B Lydian, A♭ Dorian, D Phrygian, and B♭ Mixolydian. You may use key signatures or accidentals.

3. Construct three cadences in each mode, using a variety of soprano lines, chord formulas, and textures.

4. Compose a brief piece for piano. Start in G Dorian, move to G Phrygian, and then move back to G Dorian.

5. Compose a brief piece for an instrumental combination available in class. Start in C Lydian, move to D Lydian, and then move back to C Lydian.

6. Write piano or instrumental accompaniments for the following Appalachian folk melodies. Keep the accompaniments basically simple, with a moderate to slow harmonic rhythm. Use the texture that seems to best complement the melody.

a.

b.

c.

7. Harmonize the following melodies, arranging them for combinations of instruments available in class. Employ the harmonic vocabulary and technique associated with modal music.

a.

Animé

b.

Bewegt

c.

Dolce

d.

Frisch

e.

Leggiero

6 Pandiatonicism

I. *Pandiatonic* (freely diatonic) *music* uses traditional scalar materials, but in somewhat nontraditional ways. In this technique any note of the prevailing scale—most often simply a major scale or diatonic mode—may be combined with any other notes of that scale if the result is pleasing to the composer. Any kind of chord construction may be used, although tertian sonorities are most typical. Tritone relationships are usually avoided, and chromaticism is minimal. The key is firmly established. The most common types of pandiatonic use follow.

A. The composer may use nontraditional arrangements of scalar notes; chords can be understood as tall chords, added note chords, or suspensive chords.

[C6(add9) Dm7 Em7(add4) Fmaj9 G9 Am7 Cmaj7 Fmaj9 Em7(add 4) Dm7]

B. The composer may use tall or additive tertian sonorities, often associated with pedal effects and typically dominant.

[C: dominant pedal]

C. The composer may use chordal ostinato effects, usually involving alternation of two or three chords.

D. The composer may use two contrapuntal "streams" of chords, often resulting in a polychordal sound (see Part IV, Unit 9).

II. Suggestions for class discussion.

    A. Analyze the examples as discussed in paragraph I.

    B. Analyze the examples in Unit 32 of *Music for Analysis*. Students may bring additional examples from the literature into class.

    C. Suggested reading (see the Bibliography): Dallin, Persichetti, Reti, Ulehla.

eWorkbook exercises, online tutorials, and musical examples with audio for this unit are available at the *Techniques and Materials of Music* website, **TMMTheory.com**.

Visit the
TMM website

Exercises

1. Study the Ravel *Mother Goose Suite: The Magic Garden* (#402 in *Music for Analysis*). Then, write six to eight measures in the style of Example I–A.

2. Write two phrases for piano employing pedal effects, as in Example I–B.

3. Continue and complete Example I–D for brass choir.

4. Write a brief choral "Amen," starting as follows:

5. Complete the following fanfare for brass choir:

6. Harmonize the following using a pandiatonic idiom. Strive for an effective accompanimental pattern, possibly an ostinato. Experiment with a variety of devices such as added notes, interior pedal points, and so forth. This may be written for piano or instruments available in class.

7 Exotic (Artificial, Synthetic) Scales

I. Scale forms other than traditional major, minor, and church modes are known as *exotic*, *artificial*, or *synthetic scales*. Some are derived from folk music, some come from cultures other than Western, and some are constructed by composers to yield special interval relationships. These scale forms may be built on any pitches. Among the most common scales in these categories are the following:

II. Any arrangement of two to twelve notes of the tempered scale may constitute a scale, although most exotic, artificial, and synthetic scales contain five to eight tones. Each scale tends to emphasize certain intervals and may completely lack other intervals. For example, the whole-tone scale, rich in M2, M3, and A4 (and their inversions), lacks m2, m3, and P4 (and their inversions). The pentatonic scale lacks m2 and A4. Interval content may affect the choice of transposition. All scales are abstractions; they are merely conventionally arranged collections of notes from which the composer may select in writing music. Composers occasionally employ nonconventional key signatures when exotic or artificial scales are consistently used.

A. In composing with these scales it is important to emphasize the characteristic intervals within each scale, as well as to emphasize clearly the tonic note by the usual means of reiteration, return, line emphasis, and appropriate cadence formulas.

B. Scales often consist of two equivalent *tetrachords* (sets of four adjacent pitches), as in the major scale and the octatonic and Hungarian minor variant. As with the modes, it is possible to change scales over a single tonic or to transpose a scale to a new tonic for variety. Scales may be mixed freely within a given passage or used simultaneously. Frequently, the tetrachords may be extracted and used independently.

C. The transposition factor applies to composition with exotic scales. Refer to Part IV, Unit 1, for an explanation and examples.

III. *Scale and chord.* Exotic scales will frequently generate particular types of chord structures.

A. A pentatonic scale projected as a chord will result in either an additive chord or a quartal (or quintal) stack.

B. The whole-tone scale will generate (1) augmented triads, (2) altered dominants (whole-tone dominants), and (3) clusters.

C. The octatonic scale is rich in triads, dominant seventh chords, diminished seventh chords, and polychordal combinations (see Unit 9).

IV. Suggestions for class discussion.

    A. Analyze the examples in Unit 33 of *Music for Analysis*. Students may bring additional examples from the literature into class.

    B. Analyze the interval content of pentatonic, octatonic, and whole-tone scales. Which intervals are present? Which are missing? Which transpositions will introduce an entirely new set of notes? Which other transpositions will introduce certain notes in common with the original scale? How can these facts be used to create musical interest?

    C. Suggested reading (see the Bibliography): Dallin, Hanson, Persichetti, Ulehla.

Visit the
TMM website

eWorkbook exercises, online tutorials, and musical examples with audio for this unit are available at the *Techniques and Materials of Music* website, **TMMTheory.com**.

Exercises

1. Construct five artificial scales consisting of five to nine tones that emphasize certain intervals and avoid others.

2. Compose a brief work for instruments available in class, based on one of the scales from Exercise 1.

3. Employing the scale demonstrated in II–A, write a brief work for piano.

4. Write accompaniments for the following pentatonic melodies. Experiment with different harmonic structures and different textures. Try using melodic or chordal ostinatos. Also

consider harmonizing the melodies with tones restricted to the tones of the pentatonic scale. Analyze the resulting chord structures.

a.

5. Determine the scale of the given material, and then complete, adding six to eight measures:

a.

b.

c.

8 Quartal and Secondal Harmony

I. Chords may be constructed of intervals other than thirds; fourths, fifths, or seconds are frequently used. Perfect fourths may be superimposed or combined with augmented fourths. Perfect or diminished fifths can also be used.

II. The use of the Hanson, Persichetti, and Hindemith systems is appropriate in the analysis of quartal and secondal harmony. (See Part IV, Unit 2.)

$p^4mn^2s^3$

       Hanson   Persichetti   Hindemith

III. Secondal sonorities are often the result of closely spaced quartal or tertian chords. The effect of a sonority results not so much from the intervals it contains as from the spacing of these intervals. Thick secondal sonorities are usually termed *clusters*.

IV. Because traditional chord names do not apply to nontertian harmony, the following terminology is suggested:

Number of Different Notes in a Chord	Name
2	dyad
3	triad (trichord)
4	tetrad
5	pentad
6	hexad
7	heptad

---

*For further examples of nontraditional notation, see Stone.

V. Few works are consistently quartal or secondal. Often the two types can be mixed, and both work well with tertian material, including tall chords. Quartal chords can gain greater variety by inverting the intervals they contain. (The term *inversion* does not apply here in the traditional sense, because the quality and function of quartal materials alter with rearrangement.) A four- and a three-note quartal sonority follow, each followed by chords derived through inversion:

VI. Some possible cadences follow. Note that the first two examples contain chords derived exclusively from perfect fourths. The third example contains both perfect and augmented fourths, and its final chord is a triad.

VII. *Chord and melody.* In quartal context, melodic lines will often reflect the underlying quartal harmony by using frequent leaps of fourths. Projections of fourths and sequential patterns typically result in the use of all the notes of the chromatic scale.

VIII. Suggestions for class discussion.

A. Analyze the examples in Unit 34 of *Music for Analysis*. Students may bring additional examples from the literature into class.

B. Carefully analyze the following sonorities, using any system. (See Part IV, Unit 2, for various systems.)

C. Suggested reading (see the Bibliography): Dallin, Hanson, Hindemith, Persichetti, Ulehla.

eWorkbook exercises, online tutorials, and musical examples with audio for this unit are available at the *Techniques and Materials of Music* website, **TMMTheory.com**.

Visit the
TMM website

Exercises

1. Respace and rearrange (by inversion of intervals) each of the following sonorities in at least five ways:

2. Study the Hindemith *Mathis der Maler: Grablegung* (#421 in *Music for Analysis*). Then, analyze the given chords in the following and continue harmonizing using the same vocabulary.

    a.

    b.

3. Continue the following for ten to fifteen measures:

4. Compose a brief work for instruments available in class, using nontertian chord structures.

9 Polyharmony and Polytonality

I. *Polyharmony* involves the simultaneous sounding of two or more tertian chords with distinct roots *(polychords)*. The variables are the quality of the chords, the root relationships, and the spacing or arrangement of the chords. Polychords may be used within a diatonic context (Example a) or a chromatic context (Example b). Note the analysis.

a.

b.

$$\frac{G}{C} \quad \frac{C}{F} \qquad \frac{F}{Em} \quad \frac{C}{Dm}$$

$$\frac{E}{C} \quad \frac{F\sharp}{D} \quad \frac{G}{E} \qquad \frac{D\flat}{F}$$

Chords most often used are major, minor, Mm7, and MM7. Roots may all be similarly related, or there may be no system for root selection.

$$\frac{Em}{Dm} \qquad \frac{D}{C} \quad \frac{C\sharp m7}{Bm7} \qquad \frac{E\flat maj7}{A\flat maj7}$$

The chords in a polychord are kept distinct by spacing, by placing the chords in contrapuntal "streams," or by contrasting orchestration; otherwise, certain spacings will be ambiguous. For example, is apt to sound like a tall chord, whereas will sound like a cluster.

223

Polychords may also be expressed in linear fashion:

$$\frac{D}{B\flat} \qquad \frac{E}{C} \qquad \frac{G}{E\flat} \qquad \frac{A}{F}$$

II. *Chord and scale.* Diatonic polychords will typically reduce to a simple diatonic scale (major or church mode), and the effect is often like pandiatonicism. Chromatic polychords may reduce to a single exotic scale, frequently octatonic.

Stravinsky

III. *Polytonality* involves the simultaneous sounding of two or more distinct areas of tonality, expressed as lines or chords. The variables are the scale or mode of each element and the relationship of the tonics. Traditional scalar materials are usually used. Each scalar element must be kept distinct by spacing or orchestration.

Tonal areas can be made distinct from one another by selecting keys with the most distant tonal relationships to provide the fewest common notes between scales. Occasionally, however, the composer will choose scales that provide for common tones; the result is very similar to a synthetic scale or a permutational scale, in which certain tones occur in both raised and lowered form.

The following example is both polychordal and polytonal:

Pomposo

D:	D	C#°	Bm	A	G
B♭:	B♭		E♭		F

Polytonal passages are usually resolved in one of two ways: into a sonority containing elements of both keys or into a single key. Polytonal material is often used in brief, isolated passages.

IV. Suggestions for class discussion.

A. Analyze the examples in Unit 35 of *Music for Analysis*. Students may bring additional examples from the literature into class.

B. Experiment with polychords, trying major triads in various root relationships and spacings. Also try MM7 and MMM9 chords.

C. Analyze several polychordal examples. What root relationships are used? Is there a clear rationale for the chord successions and/or root relationships? What qualities of triads seem to work best together?

D. Suggested reading (see the Bibliography): Dallin, Persichetti, Ulehla.

Visit the
TMM website

eWorkbook exercises, online tutorials, and musical examples with audio for this unit are available at the *Techniques and Materials of Music* website, **TMMTheory.com**.

Exercises

1. Experiment with polytonality. Set up a simple accompaniment pattern, keeping to a single tonal area. Write a melody against it that begins in the same key, moves through distinctly contrasting keys, and then returns to the original key.

2. Write brief passages for piano that illustrate the following:

    a. Diatonic polychords within G major, using nonsystematic root relationships.
    b. Chromatic polychords, using systematic root relationships and/or exact planing.

3. Write a two-voice contrapuntal example using a polyharmonic chordal basis.

4. Write a two-voice example using two modes or synthetic scales having some common tones. If possible, use different key signatures or partial signatures for each voice (in the style of Bartók).

5. Analyze the given material, and complete in the same idiom:

a.

b.

6. Study the excerpt from Honegger *Symphony No. 5* (#432 in *Music for Analysis*). Then, continue harmonizing the following melody employing chromatic polychords.

10 Free Atonality and Set Theory

I. Much contemporary music is conceived in terms of the manipulation of a restricted set of intervals instead of scale forms, traditional materials, or serial processes. In this procedure a basic interval *cell* (or *set*) may give rise to a whole work, in both its harmonic and linear aspects. The cell itself may be treated as a motive. A cellular approach typifies much serial music (see Part IV, Unit 11). Much music of this type is not strongly centric and is frequently termed *atonal*.

II. Characteristic procedures.

A. The basic cell, or set of interval relationships, may be altered in any of the following ways:

| set | inversion | transposition | expansion | contraction | mirroring |
| 1 | 2 | 3 | 4 | 5 | 6 |

B. The cell is usually applied to both the vertical and horizontal aspects and often accounts for most of the sounds heard in a work. The following excerpt uses the first five of the derivations in example in II–A.

C. Many interesting chords can be built by projecting two or more different intervals in succession. In such sonorities, note duplication at the octave or fifteenth is usually avoided. Melodic lines may be derived from any of the resultant sonorities.

M3, m3   P4, A4   P5, M3   (line derived from 3)

III. The transposition factor is especially relevant to interval music. Any set lacking a given interval or its inversion may be transposed by that interval, yielding pitches not contained in the original set.

set | set | set
(contains no major thirds) | (transposed down a major third) *or* | (transposed up a major third)

IV. *Pitch-class set* analysis provides another tool for analyzing complex pitch structures or for discovering relationships in the music that might not be readily apparent. *Pitch-class* refers collectively to all the occurrences of a particular pitch, regardless of register. Pitches spelled enharmonically are to be considered as the same pitch. Pitch-class sets consist of from three to twelve pitch-classes. They may occur as melodic motives or gestures, as vertical sonorities, or as combinations, or they may be noncontiguous but related by register, metrical placement, or the like. Since smaller sets are easier to work with, the music is typically *segmented*. This process breaks longer musical figures into manageable groupings.

Schoenberg, op. 19, no. 2

Sets can be further divided into *subsets:*

To analyze a pitch-class set, first write the selected pitches in scalar order within the octave. Consider that in dealing with atonal music two basic assumptions are routinely made: 1. Enharmonic spellings are considered to be equivalent, and spelling may be changed to make the intervals simpler. 2. Any interval and its inversion are considered to be equivalent, and therefore intervals are reduced to their smaller size. The pitch-class set is first put into *normal order*, as described above, and because it is also useful to consider pitch-class sets and their inversions to be equivalent, the set is ultimately reduced to what is termed *lowest ordering* or the *best normal order*. Finding the normal order may require some rotation of the pitches to assure the proper ordering, with the smaller intervals to the left and the larger intervals to the right, and the smallest possible interval from first note to last. The pitches are then numbered, with the first note being the integer 0, and the following notes numbered according to the number of semi-tones above the first pitch. The pitch-class integers are separated by commas, and the series of numbers is placed in brackets. The resulting integer series becomes the label for the set: [0,1,4], [0,3,4,7], and so on. The set may then be transposed so that the first note is middle c; this puts the set into *prime form* or *prime order*. Allen Forte determined that there are only 220 possible sets, and he has indexed all of these sets, providing them with convenient index numbers: [0,1,4] = Set 3-3; [0,3,4,7] = Set 4-17; and so on.

The use of the commas avoids confusion when using the integers 10 and 11. Some theorists prefer to use letters for these integers so that the commas can be eliminated. T (or A) stands for 10, and E (or B) stands for 11. Thus, the set [0,2,5,8,10] can be written [0258T].

Conventional structures can also be given a set designation.

Bartók, op. 6, no. 10

[0,2,4,6,8,10]
Forte index 6-35

[0,2,4,6,8,10]
Interval vector: [060603]

For example, [0,2,4,6,8,10] is a whole-tone scale. Other aspects of the set can be seen by examining the interval vector, which is a tabulation of the total number of intervals within the set. The vector consists of six digits, also placed within brackets. Each digit represents an *interval class.* The first digit represents the number of m2s or M7s, the second digit represents the number of M2s or m7s, the third the number of m3s or M6s, the fourth the number of M3s or m6s, the fifth the number of P4s or P5s, and the last the number of tritones. An examination of the interval vector for this set reveals that it is rich in M2s, M3s, and tritones, as we would expect of a whole-tone scale, but lacking in all other intervals.

Visit the TMM website

For eWorkbook exercises, musical examples, a tutorial, and a quiz on music analysis with sets, visit the *Techniques and Materials of Music* website at **TMMTheory.com**.

V. Suggestions for class discussion.

A. Analyze the examples in Unit 36 of *Music for Analysis.* Students may bring additional examples from the literature into class.

B. Suggested reading (see the Bibliography): Cope, Dallin, Forte, Hanson, Persichetti, Ulehla, DeLone.

Exercises

1. Reduce each of the following examples to its pitch-class set, and analyze the resulting set.

2. Experiment with building massive dissonant sonorities by projecting in alternation two or three different intervals, as suggested in II–C. Analyze the results using the Hanson system or some other method of interval analysis.

3. Build several chords by mirroring around a central note. Analyze according to the instructions for Exercise 2.

4. Compose a brief work for piano based on the interval set G–Bb–C–F♯. Derive both melody and harmony from the set and its transpositions. Try to construct a convincing cadence.

5. Study the Bartok *Mikrokosmos, no. 144: Minor Seconds, Major Sevenths* (#444 in *Music for Analysis*). Then, compose a short work for instruments available in class using the basic cell of the example in II–A.

6. Analyze the given material, and continue in the same idiom:

a.

b.

c.

11 Twelve-Tone Serialism

I. Serial procedures can become complex, but the basic principles are simple.

A. In *twelve-tone serialism*, a *tone-row* (set, or *row* for short) of twelve different *pitch-classes** (p.c.'s) is set up to control relationships. Pitches may be sounded in succession (melodically) or simultaneously (harmonically) and may be sounded in any octave. Notes may be repeated directly, but no pitch-class may be reused until the entire row has been sounded. Rows may be broken down into two groups of six notes each (hexachords) or three groups of four notes each (tetrachords). Divisions into three-note groups and even two-note groups are also found.

In serial music, the row will "control" the whole work, in both its harmonic and linear aspects. A single statement of the row may coincide with a phrase, or statements of the row may be independent of formal structure, though row forms and variants or particular transpositions may be used to define contrasting sections of larger movements.

B. Four forms of the row are available: Prime (P_0), Inversion (I_0), Retrograde (R_0), and Retrograde Inversion (RI_0).

C. Any of the four basic forms may be transposed, giving a total of forty-eight possible associated sets. The level of transposition is indicated by the small number following the initial designating the form of the row. This number indicates the number of semi-tones above the reference pitch. Thus, P_6 indicates the prime form of the row transposed up a tritone (six semi-tones higher). The reference pitch for transpositions of P and I forms is the first pitch-class of P_0; the reference pitch for transpositions of R and RI forms is the first or last pitch-class of R_0.

---

*See Part IV, Unit 2, I, and Part IV, Unit 10, IV.

Much serial music employs the convention of using an accidental, including the natural sign, before each note. In this case, the accidental refers *only* to that note and does not carry through the measure.

Compared with traditional common practice tonal theory, the field of post-tonal analysis is relatively new. Accordingly, there are a number of approaches and analytic systems that differ in their details, and new approaches are being proposed every year. We have tried to present all the alternatives so that instructors can choose which method they find most congenial.

In the analysis of serial music, the row-forms are first identified, their transposition levels determined, and the sequence of pitches numbered. The pitch series may be numbered from 1 to 12, though some analysts prefer to number the series from 0 to 11. (The pitch-classes in the series may also be designated by their pitch-class numbers, where c = 0.) There is also some disagreement about the numbering, and thus the transposition level, of R and RI forms. If one considers R to be simply the retrograde of P, there is a certain symmetry in numbering the R form from 12 to 1 and calculating transposition level by comparing note 1 to note 1. Similarly, RI may be considered simply the reverse of I, and the series numbered from 12 to 1. Some analysts prefer to number all row-forms from 1, and thus the transposition level of R and RI forms will vary, depending on the system employed.

That form of the row designated as P_0 has traditionally been designated rather arbitrarily as the first row-form to appear in a given piece or section of a piece. There is, of course, no way of knowing for certain whether this was actually the row that the composer constructed as the basis for the piece. Analysts often simply designate the P_0 form as the transposition level that would begin on the note c. In this system, the prime form of the Schoenberg row presented above would be designated as P_2.

It is important to keep in mind that analyzing the row-forms is only the beginning of analysis of a serial piece. All of the other aspects of music—texture, motive, recurrence, and manipulation of musical gestures or figures, and the like—should always be considered.

D. It is often helpful in analyzing or composing serial works to construct a *matrix (magic square)*, containing all the possible rows derived from (associates of) the prime row. In constructing such a matrix, the P_0 is first written across the page, then the I_0 is written down from the first note of P_0. At this point the rest of the P row-forms can be written, left to right, starting from each note of the I-forms. The R and RI forms will result automatically: the R forms are read from right to left, and the RI forms from bottom to top.

The following matrix is for the Gavotte from Schoenberg's Suite, op. 25.

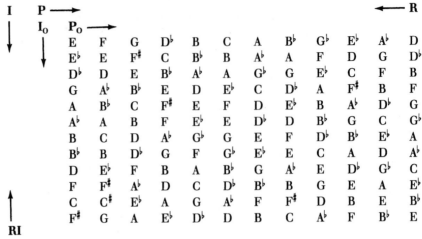

	P₀ →										
	E	F	G	D♭	B	C	A	B♭	G♭	E♭	A♭	D
	E♭	E	F♯	C	B♭	B	A♭	A	F	D	G	D♭
	D♭	D	E	B♭	A♭	A	G♭	G	E♭	C	F	B
	G	A♭	B♭	E	D	E♭	C	D♭	A	F♯	B	F
	A	B♭	C	F♯	E	F	D	E♭	B	A♭	D♭	G
	A♭	A	B	F	E♭	E	D♭	D	B♭	G	C	G♭
	B	C	D	A♭	G♭	G	E	F	D♭	B♭	E♭	A
	B♭	B	D♭	G	F	G♭	E♭	E	C	A	D	A♭
	D	E♭	F	B	A	B♭	G	A♭	E	D♭	G♭	C
	F	F♯	A♭	D	C	D♭	B♭	B	G	E	A	E♭
	C	C♯	E♭	A	G	A♭	F	F♯	D	B	E	B♭
	F♯	G	A	E♭	D♭	D	B	C	A♭	F	B♭	E

I — P →   ← R   (RI vertical arrows surrounding matrix)

II. Some principal variation techniques.

A. Any two or more tone-row forms may be used simultaneously.

B. The principle of strict succession may be varied by ostinatos, trills, repeated notes, pedal effects, tremolos, or chords.

C. *Segmentation* involves the partitioning of 12 tone sets into *subsets* or *segments*, usually into hexachords (6 p.c.'s) or trichords (3 p.c.'s), which are often used somewhat independently of each other in a given work. Schoenberg's technique typically involves independent hexachords; Webern often works with trichords. In a derived set (see the Webern example under III), permutations of the first trichord of a set give rise to the subsequent trichords.

III. A multitude of different rows is possible. The composer constructs or selects a basic row on the basis of the particular interval characteristics it exhibits and selects from the forty-eight forms those few that yield the interval or pitch relationships to be exploited. All forty-eight forms are rarely used in a single work. Most serial music is clearly not strongly centric, but there is no reason why it cannot be. Some rows are very traditional in effect, such as the following Berg example; others (Nono, Webern) are less so.

Rows of fewer than twelve notes may be used.

IV. Row-forms and transposition levels are determined by a number of considerations. A particular transposition may result in the pitch-classes associated with certain intervals remaining the same. These intervals are called *invariants* and can be of great use in establishing the relationship among row-forms or as a means of unification.

Schoenberg, Op. 25

A composer may desire a high degree of invariance or no invariance at all.

Certain rows are structured in such a way that a specific transposition or permutation of the first hexachord will produce the complementary pitch-classes, that is, the pitch-classes of the second hexachord. This means that the hexachords of the two row forms can be combined to produce the total chromatic. Rows of this kind are called *combinatorial*. Smaller segments may also be combinatorial. The Webern example cited above is an all-combinatorial row.

Combinatorality is another factor that composers may use in narrowing the choice of row-forms or transpositions from among all the possible row-forms available. Like invariants, combinatorial rows provide for greater unity and coherence.

Babbit *Duet*

V. In *integral serialism* (total serialism, total organization), elements in addition to pitch are organized in terms of numerical series.

VI. Suggestions for class discussion.

A. Analyze the examples in Unit 37 of *Music for Analysis*. Students may bring additional examples from the literature into class.

B. Analyze all the rows given in III for interval content. Discuss the construction of these rows.

C. How can the mathematical theory of sets (groups) be used to write or analyze serial music?

D. Suggested reading (see the Bibliography): Brindle, Cope, Dallin, Forte, Perle, Persichetti, Reti, Ulehla, DeLone.

For eWorkbook exercises, a tutorial, and a quiz on twelve-tone serialism, visit the *Techniques and Materials of Music* website at **TMMTheory.com**.

Visit the
TMM website

Exercises

1. Study the Krenek *Dancing Toys, op. 83, no. 1* (#448 in *Music for Analysis*). Then, write a brief work for piano, using only the basic row form (P_0) shown in I–C.

2. Using the three rows illustrated in III, write excerpts for piano. Note the resulting interval relationships, especially the interval content of chords formed from the rows.

3. Write original rows in the following ways:

a. Construct a row to achieve maximum variety in interval relationships.
b. Construct a row to achieve minimum variety in interval relationships.

4. Analyze the serial and intervallic structure of the given material, and continue or complete:

a.

b.

See the first row under III.

c.

Note: Each accidental affects only the note immediately following it.

d. Compose a short work for piano based on this opening (see the Babbitt *Duet* row on page 236).

5. Study several examples of integral serialism, noting how aspects in addition to pitch are controlled by series processes. Then, compose a short piece for instruments in class in which such aspects as rhythm (duration and/or attack points), dynamics, registral placement, and perhaps choice of instruments are controlled by a six- or twelve-note numeric series.

12 Additional Contemporary Procedures*

I. A degree of chance is inherent in all music; this is caused by the imperfections of notation and performance variables. Baroque music, like much jazz, introduces a number of partially controlled elements (ornamentation, tempo fluctuations, and figured-bass improvisation). All live performance introduces unpredictable elements. Some recent composers have systematically introduced *random (aleatoric) elements* into their music, with some exerting only minimal control over the result and others determining all but a few details.

A. Indeterminate elements often result from practical considerations. For example, if the composer has in mind only the following generally fast, disjunct fragment that accelerates,

it may be more efficient to notate it in *proportional notation.*

Frame notation can also be used.

(play in random order)

---

*For further examples of nontraditional notation, see Stone.

238

B. The composer may leave the overall form of a work up to the performers, who are given only the details and told to play them in any order. Alternatively, the composer may predetermine the form and leave a few (or many) details somewhat (or very) open.

C. The composer must decide what elements he or she wants to control, how and to what extent they may be controlled, and how to notate the desired effect precisely.

II. In some recent music, called *texture music*, sonority has become the primary compositional consideration. Typically, this music involves clusters of varying density, dynamics, and color, as well as unusual uses of traditional instruments and nontraditional sound sources. Traditional concern with line, pitch, rhythm and meter, and harmonic progression tends to be subordinated or eliminated.

III. *Minimalism* is characterized by severe restriction of materials (pitch, rhythm, color, density, and register). Repetition with slight variations is the main device. The music unfolds through the addition of new strands or layers, as well as rhythmic phase relationships.

IV. Electronic music is a major area of contemporary musical practice that, because of its highly specialized and technical nature, is beyond the framework of this text. Useful studies for the beginning student may be found in the books listed in the Bibliography under Electronic Music.

V. Suggestions for class discussion.

A. Analyze the examples in Unit 38 of *Music for Analysis*. Students may bring additional examples from the literature into class.

B. Discuss chance elements in traditional music.

C. Discuss the æsthetic implications of chance procedures and minimalism.

D. Analyze examples of texture music and pieces using aleatoric processes. What notational and calligraphic devices are employed? To what degree is traditional notation still employed? What unusual sound resources and techniques are used?

E. Suggested reading (see the Bibliography): Cope, Forte, Nyman, Delone.

Visit the
TMM website

eWorkbook exercises, online tutorials, and musical examples with audio for this unit are available at the *Techniques and Materials of Music* website, **TMMTheory.com**.

Exercises

1. Write a piece for the class to perform, using the techniques of minimalism.

2. Write a piece for the class in which the overall form is predetermined and the details left open; then write a piece using the opposite approach.

3. Construct an ensemble piece in which fragments in frame notation can be arbitrarily ordered and combined.

4. Study the Crumb *Madrigals, Book IV* (#455 in *Music for Analysis*). Then, write a piece using proportional notation for instruments available in class.

PART 5

Reference Materials

Musical Calligraphy

Common calligraphic errors (numbers refer to items in the checklist for musical calligraphy):

Corrected example:

I. Checklist for musical calligraphy.

1. Note heads are filled in where needed and are large enough to fill the space.
2. Stems are vertical, thin, connected to heads and beams, going in proper direction, and on the proper side of the note head.
3. Beams are thick and straight, following the direction of the beamed group.
4. Alignment is perfect within each beat, and beats are evenly distributed in each bar; all beats are accounted for by notes or rests.
5. Bar lines are thick, straight, and vertical; they are laid out beforehand to fill the page.
6. Editing is full and specific; tempo, phrasing, and dynamics are included.
7. A brace is needed for the great staff.
8. The meter signature appears only at the beginning, unless the meter changes during the piece.
9. The clef and key signature must be repeated at the beginning of each staff.

II. Equipment.

    A. Fountain-type pen with a broad nib, special music pen, black felt-tip pen, or soft pencil.

    B. Black ink (for example, Pelikan Fount India or Higgins Eternal).

    C. Good-quality manuscript paper.

    D. Ruler.

    E. Ink eraser or single-edged razor blade.

III. Several good music manuscript manuals are available.

IV. Students may wish to use notation software with their computer. Most software programs not only produce print-quality notation but also allow the students to listen to their work by playing back the music entries either through the computer's own speakers or through a MIDI system. While the authors recognize that many students now use computer notation programs such as Finale and Sibelius for music copying, we feel it is still important for a musician to understand and be able to produce correct, clear musical notation by hand.

The Harmonic Series

fundamental	1	2	3	4	5	6	7	8	9	10	11	(overtones)
	1st	2nd	3rd	4th	5th	6th	7th	8th	9th	10th	11th	12th (partials)

A vibrating body, such as an air column or string, vibrates not only over its entire available length (producing the fundamental *frequency*, perceived as pitch), but also in fractional parts (one-half of its length, one-third of its length, and so on), which produces *overtones*. These overtones, or *harmonics*, are too weak in volume (*amplitude*) to be heard as individual pitches, but they do contribute to the color (timbre) of the sound. The overtones are usually multiples of the frequency of the fundamental, except with very complex sounds. For instance, with a fundamental of 100 vibrations (cycles) per second, the first overtone has 200 cycles per second (sounding one octave higher); the second overtone, 300 cycles per second (sounding a twelfth higher); the third, 400 cycles per second (sounding two octaves higher); and so on.

Note that the fundamental is also termed the first partial, resulting in a discrepancy of numbering between overtones and partials.

---

*These tones are significantly out of tune compared to the tempered system.

Nonharmonic (Nonchord) Tones

Any note that is not heard as a member of the prevailing harmony (chord) at any given time is defined as a *nonharmonic (nonchord) tone*. In some highly dissonant contemporary styles this concept is inapplicable. The following are the most common types of nonharmonic tones:

I. A *passing tone* (p.t.) is used stepwise to fill in the gaps between chord tones in a line. These may be accented or unaccented. The example in I–C is often analyzed as an appoggiatura because it is longer than its resolution and appears on a strong beat.

II. An *auxiliary tone* (aux., or *neighbor tone*) is used between a chord tone and its repetition. It may or may not be accented or in pairs, as it is in II–C.

III. An *escape tone* (e.t., or *échappée*) is unaccented, approached by step, and resolved by skip.

IV. A *free neighbor* (f.n., or *incomplete neighbor tone*) is unaccented, approached by skip, and left by step, usually in the opposite direction. It can be thought of as an unaccented appoggiatura.

V. An *anticipation* (ant.) is unaccented, anticipates a chord tone, and is usually shorter than this tone. It is typically a cadential idiom.

VI. A *pedal tone* (ped., or *pedal point*) is of long duration; it is prepared and resolved on the same pitch. A pedal tone is usually on the tonic or dominant note and serves to prolong that harmony through a passage, in which case the other voices sound like decorations of that harmony.

VII. An *appoggiatura* (app., or *"leaning note"*) is accented, approached by skip, and resolved by step, usually in the opposite direction. It is often longer than its resolution. The example in VII–C may be analyzed as an accented passing tone.

VIII. A *suspension* (sus.) is accented, prepared by a chord tone on the same pitch, and resolved by step. The suspension figure requires preparation (prep.) on a chord tone, dissonance (diss.) on a relatively strong beat, and resolution (res.) by step to a chord tone. The upward-resolving suspension is sometimes called a *retardation*. The suspension does not have to be tied from its preparation. The arabic numerals (in the following example) are used to classify suspension figures, and refer to the interval formed between the bass and the suspending voice on the suspension and resolution beats. The following idioms are common harmonic contexts for the suspension figure:

The resolution may be ornamented (VIII–A), or the chord may be changed at the point of resolution (VIII–B).

4 Relative and Linear Motion

I. *Relative motion* is the directional relationship between two voices.

   A. In *similar motion,* voices move in the same direction.

   B. In *contrary motion,* voices move in opposite directions.

   C. In *oblique motion,* one voice moves while the other remains stationary.

   D. In *parallel motion,* voices move in the same direction by the same interval.

II. *Linear motion* is melodic motion found within a single voice.

   A. In *conjunct motion,* notes move by step.

   B. In *disjunct motion,* notes move by skip.

5

Guidelines for Voice Leading in Strict Four-Part Writing

In freer textural and stylistic situations, the following guidelines for voice leading in strict four-part writing may be applied less strictly.

I. Avoid crossing and overlapping voices.

II. Avoid parallel fifths and octaves, as well as octaves or fifths by contrary motion.

III. Avoid leaps in similar motion to octaves or fifths in the outer voices, except in chord repetition. (These are termed *direct* or *hidden fifths* or *octaves*.)

IV. Do not allow three voices to leap in the same direction unless the fourth voice remains stationary or moves in contrary motion, except in chord repetition. (See the example in III.)

V. Avoid a diminished fifth moving to a perfect fifth in the outer voices (unequal fifths). However, a perfect fifth may move to a diminished fifth if the diminished fifth is subsequently resolved.

VI. In connecting chords a second apart, both of which are in root position, make the outer voices move in contrary motion. This procedure will also hold true when the bass moves by the interval of a second, as when one of the chords is in inversion, with the exception of consecutive first-inversion chords.

VII. Avoid the augmented second melodically when involved with a change of chord.

VIII. Avoid the melodic tritone (T) unless properly resolved or part of the same chord.

IX. Strive for basically conjunct motion in the upper voices.

X. Try to maintain consistent spacing within a phrase. Changes in spacing should be made only when warranted by such considerations as a wide leap in the soprano. In that case, the spacing change will allow for smoother voice leading in the interior voices.

6 Guidelines for Doubling in Strict Four-Part Writing

I. Avoid doubling tendency tones (leading tones or chord sevenths).

II. Doubling should clearly establish the function of the chord: roots first, fifths next, and thirds last. Linear considerations always take precedence.

III. Chord fifths occasionally may be omitted. When this occurs, the root may be tripled. In the case of four-tone chords, the root may be doubled.

IV. Chord thirds are rarely omitted in predominantly chordal textures.

V. Summary:

Chord	Preference for Doubling
major and minor triads in root position	root, fifth, third
tonic, subdominant, and dominant triads in first inversion	root, fifth, third
supertonic, submediant, and mediant triads in first inversion	third, root, fifth
diminished and augmented triads in root position or first inversion	third, root

VI. Scale-degrees 1, 4, and 5 are most often doubled; 2, 3, and 6, less so; and the leading tone, very rarely.

7 Checklist for Part-Writing

Students are urged to check all written work systematically as they write it, both for musicality and for technique. All work must be played or sung after completion. Some of the following items apply only at the later stages of study.

I. Play or sing each voice as you write it to check the *line* for the following:

   A. Voices are smooth and directional.

   B. There are no unnecessary large leaps.

   C. There are no unresolved diminished or augmented intervals.

   D. The outer voices have a clear contour (shape).

   E. There is a reasonable range and tessitura.

   F. Idioms are appropriate to the medium.

II. To check *counterpoint*, play each pair of voices, and check for the following:

   A. No parallel fifths or octaves should occur.

   B. No hidden octaves or fifths, or unequal fifths between the outer voices, should occur.

   C. No voice crossing or overlapping.

   D. There should be a good contrapuntal relationship between the outer voices.

III. *Spacing.*

   A. Consistent spacing should exist within each phrase.

   B. No large gaps between upper voices should occur.

   C. The texture should be homogeneous.

IV. *Doubling* should be preponderantly normal except when factors of line take precedence.

V. *Calligraphy.*

   A. Editing should be complete, when appropriate.

   B. Notation should be clear.

VI. Complete *analysis* includes key, cadences, chords, nonharmonic tones, and phrase and period structure if appropriate.

8 Chord Functions in Tonal Music

I. In common practice music, chords tend to progress in consistent, and thus predictable, patterns. *Function* refers to the tendency of a chord to progress to certain other chords. This system of chord relationships is called *functional tonality*. In tonal music, the strongest scale-degrees are 1 and 5, and the harmonies built on them exert primary control over musical form. These harmonies are normally found at the crucial structural points: beginnings (I), cadential points (I, V), and endings (I). They define the harmonic goals of the phrase and major arrival points in the form of a tonal work. Subdominant (predominant or dominant preparation) harmony is also of critical importance: this class of chord is often found at climactic points in a work, setting up dominant arrivals. All other harmonies, though important for line and color, are subsidiary for defining form. The tonic, subdominant, and dominant triads are often referred to as the "primary triads." All other harmonies may be thought of as decorating or substituting for these essential harmonies. The supertonic triad will generally function as a dominant preparation, a progression analogous to IV–V. The supertonic triad may be understood as a quasi-dominant to the dominant, the descending fifth relationship corresponding to that from dominant to tonic. The submediant and mediant triads are used less frequently than the primary triads (I, IV, and V), and have less significance for the building of musical structure. They may be thought of as embellishing or substituting for the more fundamental harmonies. They are often found in sequences.

As mentioned in the text (see, for example, Part II, Unit 12), many vertical-seeming structures, when heard in context, are clearly the result of linear motion, often of simultaneous nonharmonic tones in two or more voices. Such "chords" (usually heard as passing or neighboring sonorities) are thus "linear" in origin, and should be understood as such; in this text they are analyzed in brackets.

II. In the following common diatonic chord progressions, roman numerals are shown as they occur in the major mode. The root relationships are also valid in the minor mode.

A. Dominant functions: V–I or vii°–I.

B. Dominant preparation: IV–V, ii–V, or vi–V.

C. Roots move downward by fifth (quasi-dominant) relationships: (IV–vii°)–iii–vi–ii–V–l.

D. Roots move downward by thirds: I–vi–IV–ii.

E. Roots move upward by thirds: I–iii.

F. Roots move downward by seconds: vi–V.

G. Roots move upward by seconds: I–ii, iii–IV, IV–V, V–vi, or vii°–l.

Chord Chart   **(in sequence)**

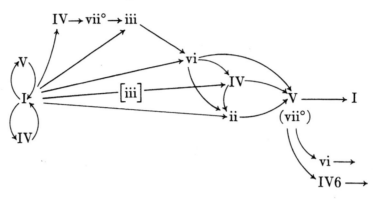

All chords are considered functional and tend to progress in the direction indicated by the arrows.

III. Chord classification system.*

Class	Diatonic Repertoire	Chromatic Repertoire
6	IV†, IV7†	secondary dominants of VII
5	vii°†, vii°7†	secondary dominants of iii
4	iii, iii7	secondary dominants of vi
3	vi, vi7	secondary dominants of ii, IV
2	ii, ii7, IV, IV7	secondary dominants of V, aug. sixths, Neapolitan chords
1	V, V7, vii°, vii°7	V7(♭5), V7(+5)

A. Types of progression.

1. *Normal progression* moves downward, class to class (iii–vi, vi–ii, and so forth).
2. *Retrogression* moves upward by skip or step (ii–vi or ii–iii).
3. *Elision* moves downward by skip (iii–IV or vi–V).

---

*The classification system suggested here follows that set out by Allen Irvine McHose in *The Contrapuntal Harmonic Technique of the Eighteenth Century* (New York: Appleton, 1947).

† In diatonic sequences only.

B. Comments on the classification system.

1. The fifth and sixth classes are rare.
2. Chords in the first and second classes and tonic predominate in most tonal styles.
3. Augmented sixth chords are sometimes found in classes other than second.
4. Ninth chords may substitute for sevenths in any class.
5. The tonic chord may normally progress to any other class.
6. The first class is commonly referred to as *dominant function*, and the second class as *dominant preparation*.
7. Movement within a class does not count as progression. Chord successions within a class often move from diatonic to chromatic or from triad to seventh chord, as in the progressions IV–V/V or ii–ii7.
8. Some of the more common elisions and retrogressions are vii°–iii, vi–V, V–vi, iii–IV, and IV—I.
9. The final goal of harmonic progression is always the tonic triad.

IV. General comments on chord progression.

A. In harmonization, a preponderance of normal progression is usually desirable.

B. In general, more than two successive nonnormal progressions should be avoided.

C. A retrogression (such as V–IV) is often followed by a normal progression back to the first chord (V–IV–V).

D. Chord change over a bar line is usually desirable.

E. Successive nonnormal progressions (V6–IV6–iii6 and so forth) are usually the result of linear activity, especially sequence.

F. Generally, the slowest harmonic rhythm appropriate to a given melody will be most effective.

G. Harmonic rhythm also depends heavily on tempo, character of the melody, and complexity of texture.

9 *Figured-Bass Symbols*

Much Baroque music is characterized by a "polarized" texture, with one or more upper voices over a bass line. This line was played by a keyboard instrument (harpsichord or organ), with one or more bass instruments (viola da gamba, cello, bass, bassoon, and so on) doubling the bass line. This practice is known as *basso continuo*, or just *continuo*, and is an essential feature of Baroque music. The middle of the texture (that is, the chords) was filled in by the keyboardist, improvising based on a system of symbols placed under the notes of the bass line. These figured-bass symbols indicated intervals and accidentals above the bass and are roughly analogous to pop or jazz chord symbols.

I. General comments on figured-bass symbols.

   A. Arabic numbers below bass notes (*figured-bass symbols*) indicate intervals formed between the bass and the upper voices.

   B. The figured-bass symbols do not indicate doubling, spacing, or compound intervals.

   C. The numbers 8, 5, and 3 do not usually appear except to cancel a previous symbol under the same bass note.

   D. The numbers 9, 7, 6, 4, and 2 must appear when needed.

II. Specific details.

   A. A bass note with no numbers indicates a root position triad, of which the given note is the root.

   B. A bass note with the numbers 6 or $\frac{6}{3}$ indicates a first-inversion triad, of which the given note is the third.

256

C. A bass note with the numbers $^6_4$ indicates a second-inversion triad, of which the given note is the fifth. The figures $^5_3$ sometimes appear next to cancel the $^6_4$, as in the progression I$^6_4$–V.

$$\begin{matrix} 6 \\ 4 \end{matrix} \longrightarrow \qquad\qquad \begin{matrix} 6 \\ 4 \end{matrix} \qquad \begin{matrix} 5 \\ 3 \end{matrix}$$

D. The figures for seventh chords are as follows.

   1. The figure 7 indicates a root-position seventh chord.

   2. The figure $^6_5$ indicates a first-inversion seventh chord.

   3. The figures $^4_3$ or $^6_{\;4}_{\;3}$ indicate a second-inversion seventh chord.

   4. The figures $^4_2$ or 2 indicate a third-inversion seventh chord.

(F: V7)   7 $\longrightarrow$ $\begin{matrix}6\\5\end{matrix}$ $\longrightarrow$ $\begin{matrix}4\\3\end{matrix}$ $\longrightarrow$ $\begin{matrix}4\\2\end{matrix}$ $\longrightarrow$

E. An accidental by itself (not immediately next to a number) in the figured bass refers to the third (or tenth or seventeenth) above the bass.

♮ $\longrightarrow$ ♯ $\longrightarrow$ ♭ $\longrightarrow$

F. Any accidental above the bass must appear in the figured-bass symbols. Alterations to the bass itself cannot appear in the symbols. Any interval above the bass can be raised or lowered by the appropriate accidental symbol.

$\begin{matrix}\cancel{8}\\(3)\end{matrix} \longrightarrow$ $\begin{matrix}\cancel{8}\\4\end{matrix}$ $\begin{matrix}\flat6\\\flat3\end{matrix}$ $\begin{matrix}\cancel{8}\\3\end{matrix}$

c: vii°$\cancel{7}$ [V$^{\cancel{6}}_{\;4}$]   G: N6   F: vii°$\cancel{7}$/ii

(b: V7)   7 $\longrightarrow$ $\begin{matrix}6\\5\end{matrix} \longrightarrow$ $\begin{matrix}\cancel{8}\\4\\3\end{matrix} \longrightarrow$ $\begin{matrix}\cancel{4}\\2\end{matrix} \longrightarrow$
          ♯

10 Procedure for Harmonizing a Figured Bass

I. Supply roman numerals.

F: I——6   vi   ii6   V   vi   V   I   V$_3^4$ I6   ii$_5^6$ [I$_4^6$]$^{cad.}$ V7   I

II. Construct the soprano melody. Be attentive to phrasing, cadences, melodic curve, and the contrapuntal relationship with the bass.

F: I——6   vi   ii6   V   vi   V   I   V$_3^4$ I6   ii$_5^6$ [I$_4^6$]$^{cad.}$ V7   I

III. Fill in the inner voices. Keep the spacing as consistent as possible and the individual lines as interesting as possible.

F: I——6   vi   ii6   V   vi   V   I   V$_3^4$ I6   ii$_5^6$ [I$_4^6$]$^{cad.}$ V7   I

IV. Add embellishments (nonharmonic tones), as appropriate, to increase musical interest and provide rhythmic continuity.

V. Rework the material in IV, employing a motivically consistent instrumental figuration. Keep the same structural elements developed in steps I through IV. This instrumental version is for woodwind quintet:

11 Procedure for Harmonizing a Melody

I. Determine the key, cadences, and phrasing. Supply roman numerals for the cadence. Where more than one chord would work well, supply both choices.

II. Supply roman numerals (*not* inversions at this point) throughout. Work for a fairly consistent harmonic rhythm. In general, the slowest harmonic rhythm (that is, speed and pattern of chord change) appropriate to the harmonic implications of the melody and the tempo will work best. Where more than one chord would work well, supply both choices. Determine which notes, if any, in the melody are to be treated as nonharmonic.

III. Construct the bass line. Be attentive to phrasing, cadences, good linear interest, and the contrapuntal relationship with the soprano melody. It is at this stage that the precise chord choices (where there is more than one possibility) and inversion choices are made.

Observe here the following:

A. The bass note changes over the bar line.

B. The harmonic rhythm reinforces the meter.

C. The harmonic rhythm is consistent in the first two measures of each phrase, quickens in the measure that precedes the cadence, and comes to rest at the cadence point.

IV. Fill in the inner voices. Keep the spacing as consistent as possible and the individual lines as interesting as possible.

V. Add embellishments (nonharmonic tones) to the lower three voices, as appropriate, to increase musical interest and rhythmic continuity. Note the consistent eighth-note motion, continuing across the bar lines and into the cadences.

VI. Rework the material in V, employing a motivically consistent instrumental figuration. Keep the same structural elements developed in steps I through V. This instrumental version is for piano:

12 Models for Expansion and Elaboration

The following procedure may be used for expansion and elaboration with the chord-phrase formats and figured or unfigured basses:

D major: **4/4** I   ii6 | cad. $\left[\text{I}_4^6\right]$ V7 | I

I. Provide outer voices.

II. Complete the basic part-writing.

III. Further expand the basic part-writing.

IV. Finally, use more textural expansion, a new soprano line, a more linear bass line, and fuller harmony. Edit completely.

13 Cadence and Phrase Structure

I. The *cadence* is one important means of formal articulation; it is a point of arrival or rest in the musical flow. Cadences may be *medial* (requiring continuation) or *final*.

  A. *Authentic cadence* (medial or final).

   1. A *perfect authentic cadence* (P.A.C.) is usually final. Its conditions follow: V (or V7)–I, both chords are in root position, and the tonic note is in the upper voice in the I chord.

   2. An *imperfect authentic cadence* (I.A.C.) is usually medial. Its conditions follow: V (V7)–I, either or both are in inversion; V (V7)–I, with a note other than the tonic note in the upper voice with the I chord; or vii° (vii°7)–I.

  B. A *half cadence* (H.C. or *semi-cadence*) is medial only and includes any cadence ending on a dominant function chord, such as IV–V, ii–V, I–V, vi–V, or V/V–V (others are possible).

  C. A *deceptive cadence* (D.C.), such as V–vi, V–IV6, or V–V7/V (others are possible), substitutes for, and is usually closely followed by, an expected authentic cadence.

  D. A *plagal cadence* (P.C.) is usually final, following an authentic cadence: IV–I, ii–I, or ii7–I.

  E. A *phrygian cadence* is the progression iv6–V♯ in a minor key, when used as a terminal progression.

II. Phrase structure and period form.

  A. A *phrase* is a musical thought ending with a partial or complete point of rest.

  B. A *period* is two phrases, usually of the same length, forming a complete musical thought. The constituent phrases normally form a question–answer (antecedent–consequent) relationship such that phrase 2 completes and complements phrase 1. The first cadence will usually be weaker than the second. The structure of the period is often as follows:

	H.C. or I.A.C.		I.A.C. or P.A.C.
Phrase 1	⌐	Phrase 2	⌐

  Periods are further classified by the motivic or melodic relationships between the two phrases. If both phrases begin with the same material, they are *similar* or *parallel*; if not, they are *contrasting*. Parallel periods most frequently state the motive at the same pitch level and with the same harmonization. Alternatively, the motive may be altered to fit a change of harmony, as, for example, when the antecedent phrase begins on tonic harmony, and the consequent begins on dominant harmony. The motive may also be stated at a new pitch level along with a change of harmony; in this instance, the period may be called a *sequential period*. If the motive is inversionally related, the period may be called an *inverted period*. Either phrase 1 or phrase 2 may be repeated, or a cadential expansion may extend phrase 2. Periods often modulate to closely related keys *(modulating period)*.

A double period consists of two consecutive periods having an antecedent–consequent relationship.

	I.A.C. or H.C.	H.C. or I.A.C.		H.C.	P.A.C.
Period 1	⌐	⌐	Period 2	⌐	⌐

The third phrase will often repeat the first phrase; the fourth phrase may repeat the second phrase but will be significantly altered to establish the necessary P.A.C.

C. A *phrase-group (phrase chain)* is a series of two or more related phrases that do not form a clear periodic structure.

14 Typical Phrase Variants

Composers generally avoid excessive regularity or squareness of phrase. Some typical variants follow.

I. Regular phrase structure can be varied through a process of inner expansion by the following means:

A. Repetition of a figure.

Capriccio — Haydn

B. Sequential expansion of a figure.

1.

String Quartet, op. 17, no. 5 — Haydn

2.

Piano Concerto, op. 58, no. 4 — Beethoven

C. Interpolation of an "extra" measure or two.

The Magic Flute, act 2, no. 18   Mozart

II. Formal elision, whereby the last beat of a phrase becomes the first beat of the following phrase, is a common device.

Piano Sonata, op. 31, no. 2   Beethoven

III. A phrase or period may be expanded at the end by several means.

A. Cadential extension, often by repeating the cadential figure following a D.C. or l.A.C.

O Cessate di Piagarmi   A. Scarlatti

B. Expansion (lengthening) of the cadential figure.

Piano Sonata, op. 2, no. 1   Beethoven

15 The Motive

I. A *motive* (M) may be defined as a relatively short musical idea that functions as a cell or basic unit from which phrases and larger structural units are constructed. The motive is characterized by its rhythmic shape, its intervals, and its harmonic implication. A motive may display only one of these characteristics (for example, rhythm alone), or it may display a combination of characteristics. The motive becomes an important unifying device either by its consistent use throughout a phrase, its use in subsequent phrases, or its use throughout an extended composition. During the course of a piece the motive may undergo considerable alteration or transformation, most frequently during transitional or developmental sections.

II. Common treatments of a motive.

    A. Repetition or recurrence.

        1. The motive may be repeated within a phrase.

Piano Sonata, op. 14, no. 2 — Beethoven

        2. The motive may appear at the beginnings of parallel phrases, transposed or untransposed.

Viola, op. 123 — Schubert

270

3. The motive may appear in accompanying voices.

"An die Musik," op. 88, no. 4 — Schubert

Du hol - de / Thou no - ble

Kunst, in wie viel grau - en Stun - den, / art, In all these man - y gray hours,

B. Change of interval.

    1. Interval changes will occur when the motive is restated at different pitch levels with the same underlying harmony.

Piano Sonata in G Minor, no. 4 — Haydn

g: i   V   i   V

Piano Sonata, K. 547a — Mozart

F: I

2. Interval changes will occur when the motive is transposed or altered to accommodate a change in the underlying harmony.

Piano Sonata in D Major, no. 37 — Haydn

Waltz, op. 9a, no. 13 — Schubert

3. Interval changes will occur when the motive is used sequentially.

The Temple of Glory — Rameau

4. A change of interval often results in a sense of motive expansion.

Piano Trio, op. 1, no. 3 — Beethoven

intervals expanded

C. Change of rhythm.

Nocturne, op. 15, no. 2 — Chopin

Piano Sonata in D Major, no. 9 — Haydn

D. Inversion.

Sonatina for Violin and Piano — Schubert

Invention no. 4, BWV 775 — Bach

E. Longer motives are frequently constructed from submotives or fragments that are "broken off" and developed separately.

Piano Concerto, K. 491 — Mozart

Piano Sonata, op. 2, no. 1   Beethoven

F. Addition of notes; transformation.

Wiegenlied, op. 49, no. 4   Brahms

Note in the following example (Rondo, K. 494) how Mozart progressively ornaments the motive, ultimately using the transformed motive in an imitative passage.

16 The Sequence

I. A *sequence* is the repetition of a musical motive or pattern on successively higher or lower pitch levels. A sequence may occur in only one voice, but most frequently it involves all voices or elements of the texture. Certain chord progressions are typically elaborated sequentially; in other instances the sequential lines themselves give rise to linear progressions (those having nonfunctional root motion).

II. Common sequential progressions.

    A. Sequences typically occur with a series of chords related by root motion of a descending fifth. When all the diatonic triads or seventh chords occur in this context, the IV and vii° will not have their more usual functions.

        1. Diatonic triads.

Piano Sonata, K. 545 — Mozart

In the minor mode, note that the VII is a major triad built on the unaltered seventh scale-degree.

Sonata in A Minor for Recorder and Continuo, no. 4 of Fifteen Solos, op. 1   Handel

2. Diatonic seventh chords.

Organ Concerto in D Minor   Vivaldi-Bach

Piano Sonatina, op. 88, no. 3

Kuhlau

C: I6 ii7 V(7) I7 IV(7) vii♯7 iii(7) vi7 ii(7) V7

3. Diatonic chords and secondary dominants in combination.

a. Nonmodulating.

Piano Sonata, K. 333, third movement

Mozart

b. Modulating.

"Danza, danza, fanciulla gentile"

Durante

dan - za,__ fan - ciul - la gen - ti - le,   al   mi - o   can - tar.
dance, maid - en __ gay,   charm -ing and sweet,   to   the   song that   I   sing.

bb: VII
f: III   VI$^6_5$ ii°   V$^6_5$ i

B. Sequences can involve linear progressions.

　　1. By thirds.

Intermezzo, op. 119, no. 3   Brahms

　　2. By seconds.

"Il nocchier nella Tempesta" from *Salustia,* act 2, scene 9   Pergolesi

pur   ta - lo - ra__   sal - vo al_____   li - do lo____   por

17 Textures

I. *Monophonic texture* consists of a single line, or lines doubled at the unison or octave, occurring for only one or two beats or for several measures:

II. *Chordal texture* consists predominantly of *block chords,* or all voices moving in the same rhythm.

    A. Simple four-voice texture.

    B. Simple three-voice texture may be considered a reduction of four-voice texture. Chords are either triads with no doublings or triads with one tone omitted and conventional doubling (for example, doubled root). Four-voice texture is often implied by skips in one or more of the lines.

C. *Multiple doublings* are one or more lines doubled at the octave, or expansion to five or more voices.*

D. Keyboard textures are often free, with the texture varying frequently, generally by "filling out" certain chords or as a result of adding or dropping lines.

III. In a solo with accompaniment, the solo element may be a single line, may be duplicated with parallel intervals, or may be harmonized in close spacing. Note that normal voice-leading procedures are followed in the accompanying voices, or the voices are implied by a broken chord pattern.

A. Simple chords.

*Much passage work in keyboard music can be related to an elaboration of multiple doublings.

B. Dance style (stride piano or "boom-chuck" patterns).

C. Broken chord patterns.

IV. *Polyphonic texture* consists of two or more equal and independent lines. Often the lowest line functions specifically as a bass line; at other times it is an equal melodic line; often it combines both aspects. Polyphonic textures often occur in alternation with chordal textures, thus providing an additional element of contrast or variety. Occasionally, one or more voices will be duplicated (harmonized) with parallel intervals.

18 An Introduction to Tonal Melody

I. Tonal melody uses three types of melodic motion: repetition of pitches, arpeggiation of triads, and stepwise (scalar) motion.

Piano Sonata in D Major, no. 9 — Haydn

Die Schöne Müllerin, op. 25, no. 2 — Schubert

Piano Trio, op. 97 — Beethoven

Piano Sonatina IV in F Major — Haydn

II. The formal structure of melody is related to the underlying harmonic framework. Cadences are an interaction of harmonic and melodic activity; harmonic goals have their counterpart in melodic goals. A melodic half cadence commonly uses either the supertonic or leading tone; a perfect authentic cadence, the tonic, and so forth.

III. The range of many melodies falls within the area bounded by the tonic and its octave or the dominant and its octave. Notes outside this area are used sparingly, with the highest and lowest notes occurring only once or twice.* The rise and fall of the line within this limit is called the *melodic curve* or *waveline*. Occasionally, a melody will exhibit a very narrow range, or static waveline, but in this case other elements (for example, contrapuntal activity or highly rhythmic character) compensate for the lack of curve.

*Important exceptions to this are found in piano and instrumental literature, especially that of a soloistic or virtuosic nature.

IV. Rhythmic motion through the phrase is achieved by using quicker notes on weak beats to carry the music across the bar line. Agogic accents (accents by duration) generally coincide with metric accents; syncopation and the use of longer notes on weak beats create variety or special effects.* Most melodies use only one or two basic rhythmic patterns or motives, with variations coming toward the cadence points, where the motion is often increased. If one phrase begins with an upbeat, so will subsequent phrases, and the upbeat figure will probably recur throughout the phrase.

Piano Trio, op. 1, no. 3　　　　　　　　　　Beethoven

V. The style characteristics of the melody are determined by the medium and purpose for which the melody is composed, the texture, and so forth, as well as by the type of expression the composer desires. The one general criterion would seem to be the unity of style. The type of expression desired plays an important role in determining the use of nonharmonic tones.

---

*Certain dances have particular patterns with a stressed second beat in triple meter, for example, the saraband and mazurka.

A. The use of simple weak passing tones and auxiliaries results in a harmonically straightforward, "masculine" line.

Sonatina for Violin and Piano, op. 137, no. 1   Schubert

B. Melodies using a large number of strong-beat nonharmonic tones have a highly expressive, "feminine" character.

Quartet, K. 428   Mozart

C. In homophonic music, if the structure of the phrase is clearly delineated by the bass line and accompaniment, the melody may exhibit greater freedom. For example, at a medial cadence the melodic activity often continues through the measure, thus creating a "melodic link" between the two phrases.

String Quartet, op. 3, no. 5   Haydn

D. In much romantic music and many slow movements of classical works, the melody often takes on a highly ornamental, elaborate, improvisatory character.

Ballade, op. 47, no. 3   Chopin

VI. Sample analysis for study.

An den Sonnenschein, op. 36, no. 4   Schumann

VII. A brief introduction to structural-pitch reduction.

Not all the pitches in a given melody or bass line are equally important. The graphic reduction of a line to its main pitches helps reveal the directional nature of the line, as well as the ways in which line and tonality interact. Although the identification of structural pitches is to some extent subjective, the notes that tend to sound most important in any given line are those that are accented and/ or long. These are often tonic triad members and goal notes.

The following structural-pitch reduction is suggested by, but not directly based on, the work of Austrian theorist Heinrich Schenker (1868–1935). The following symbols are used in this reduction:

- ♩ = principal structural pitch (tonic note)
- o = secondary pitch
- ● = decorative pitch
- ⌒ = melodic motion prolonging or connecting structural pitches; these comprise arpeggiation (A), neighboring motion (N), and passing motion (P)
- ⌒→ = prolongations and octave transfers of structural pitches

Dotted lines in this example show the basic scalar motion:

Symphony no. 104 in D Major, fourth movement   Haydn

One possible reduction follows:

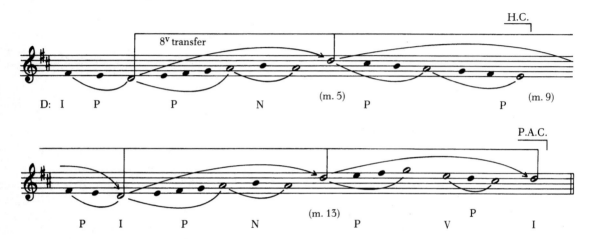

19 An Introduction to Tonal Counterpoint

I. The term *counterpoint* refers to a texture in which the voices exhibit some degree of linear independence. Most music is to some degree contrapuntal.

II. In studying the relationship between two given voices, the following items should be noted;

    A. Note the rhythmic relationship. The voices may proceed in the same note values but are more often rhythmically distinct, frequently in a ratio of 2:1.

    B. Note relative directions. The voices may run in parallel, similar, oblique, or contrary motion in relation to one another. In most pieces a mixture of all four types prevails, with a slight preference for contrary motion. Parallel perfect consonances are not found, and too many successive parallel imperfect consonances detract from the independence of line.

Bagatelle, op. 126, no. 5   Beethoven

C. Note vertical (harmonic) intervals. In general, imperfect consonances are preponderant, except at the beginning of a phrase and at cadence points, where perfect unisons, octaves, and fifths are often found. The intervals placed on the beat are usually consonant, except when a nonharmonic tone is clearly heard in one voice.

Allegro   Handel

Viennese Sonatina   Mozart

*Occasionally one or more voices will be coupled at the third or sixth.

The harmonic implications of the most common vertical intervals are as follows: thirds and sixths imply triads; seconds and sevenths imply seventh chords; and tritones imply dominant function.

D. Note *invertible counterpoint,* a technique in which the voices exchange place so that the upper voice becomes the lower.

Sonata, K. 280 — Mozart

Sonata, op. 14, no. 1 — Beethoven

Sonata, op. 13   Beethoven

E. Note melodic materials.

　　1. The voices may have different motivic material.

Tristan und Isolde, Prelude   Wagner

2. The voices may share the same motivic material.

3. *Imitation* is the technique in which the same melodic material is taken up in succession by different voices. Imitative passages are analyzed in terms of the time and pitch intervals between the voices at their entry and the length for which the imitation is carried out. For example, the following Bach invention illustrates imitation at two measures (six beats) at the octave below:

Invention in D Minor — Bach

Sonata, op. 2, no. 2 — Beethoven

Symphonic Etudes, op. 13 — Schumann

Stretto imitation occurs when the imitating voice enters before the first voice has finished its statement, as follows:

Viennese Sonatina   Mozart

Symphonic Etudes, op. 13   Schumann

Intermezzo, op. 118, no. 4   Brahms

F. Note the harmony. As in the previous examples, the underlying harmony is almost always clear and functional, often with a steady and fairly slow harmonic rhythm.

20 Form

I. *Form* in tonal music is articulated by tonal factors, cadence types and placement, motivic relationships, and sometimes by aspects of texture and color.

II. Typical formal procedures based on counterpoint:

    A. *Cantus firmus* is a procedure in which a preexisting melody is heard in relatively long tones, around which the other voices move in faster values. Most chorale preludes are of this type.

    B. *Basso ostinato* (ground bass) is a variation technique based on a repeating melodic pattern, usually heard in the lowest voice. The pattern is four, eight, or sixteen measures long; is usually in triple meter; in the minor mode; and moves between the tonic and dominant notes. Passacaglia and chaconne are two common variation forms using ostinato.

    C. A *fugue* is an extended imitative work based on one theme *(subject)*. The first section consists of an *exposition*, with alternating entrances of the subject and the *answer,* or *response,* (the subject stated at the dominant level). Statements of the subject and answer may be separated by brief linking passages *(codettas)*. There may or may not be a consistent countertheme *(countersubject)* heard with the subject. Following the exposition, the fugue alternates *episodes* (developmental sections, usually sequential and modulatory, based on motivic material from the subject) and *middle entries* of the subject and/or answer in a variety of keys. The subject usually returns in the tonic key near the end. A *double fugue* has two subjects, which are exposed either together at the beginning or in two separate expositions and combined later.

    D. An *invention* is a relatively short imitative piece based on a single melodic idea. As with the fugue, imitative statements of the principal motive alternate with episodic passages based on the motive.

III. *Binary form.*

    A. In *simple binary form*, A B, or A A′, or ‖ : A : ‖ ‖ : B : ‖, the two sections may be roughly equal in length, or the second section may be longer. The first section may modulate to a closely related key, such as the dominant or relative, and therefore is open ended, and the second remodulates to the tonic.

Minuet from Suite no. 1

Purcell

B. In *rounded binary form*, A B A′ or ‖ : A : ‖ ‖ : B A′: ‖, the first section often modulates to the dominant or relative, and the B section remodulates to tonic. The initial A section is therefore open ended, and the final A section is complete (closed ended). The B section typically develops material from the A section and either prolongs the V or ends with a half cadence. The B section is never an independent thematic unit, or closed ended, as it is in ternary forms. The two sections may be proportionally balanced, especially in those situations where B is only a single phrase and where only a single phrase of the initial A recurs in the second section. It is typical, however, to expand the second section by extending the B section and bringing back the entire initial A section, but with the harmonic progression altered to remain in the tonic key.

Sonata

Haydn

C. *Bar form* is ‖ : A : ‖ B. The B section is often as long as, or longer than, the repeated A section.

"Nun danket alle Gott"

Johann Crüger

IV. In most *three-part (ternary) forms* the sections are roughly equal in length and independent (closed ended and self-contained). The B section is usually in a closely related key.

Wichtige Begenheit, from *Kinderszenen*   Schumann

V. In *compound ternary form*, each of the three sections usually consists of a *rounded binary form*. In the following example, the "Da Capo" instruction provides the final **A** section.

Menuetto, Sonatina No. VI, from *Six Viennese Sonatinas*

Menuetto D.C.

VI. *Variation form.* Variations in the Classical period are typically based on a theme written in simple binary or (more typically) rounded binary, or (much more rarely) ternary form. Each variation will most frequently reflect the form of the theme, and these variations will be sectional or noncontinuous. Each variation also tends to retain the harmonic structure of the theme, and the variation will often be simply figurative elaboration on that progression, hence the common term *figural variations.* Some alterations to the harmonies may occur, particularly in variations in the parallel mode. The melody of the theme may be ornamented in the variations or reduced to structural pitches as the basis for new melodic figures. In the Romantic period, the variations become structurally more diverse and quite contrasting in character, with more of a reliance on the theme itself for unity. In the twentieth century, variations may be based on a theme, a chord progression, or even a series of pitches.

VII. *Sonata form* consists of three large sections: *exposition, development,* and *recapitulation.* The *exposition* consists of the following parts: the *first theme* (A) in the tonic key; the *transition,* which is modulatory; and the *second theme* (B), usually in the dominant key (if the tonic is major) or the relative key (if the tonic is minor). The *second theme* may be followed by an additional theme, or *closing theme,* also in the new key. The *exposition* may be concluded with a *codetta,* which is primarily cadential. The development section develops the material of the exposition, and possibly new material as well. Typically, the development section passes through several keys. At the end of the development there is often a *retransition;* this section reestablishes the tonic key and prepares for the recapitulation, which normally contains the material of the exposition, although with some modifications. The recapitulation normally remains in the tonic key. An *introduction* may occur at the beginning of the form, and a *coda* may occur at the end.

In the following diagram, optional elements of sonata form are presented in parentheses:

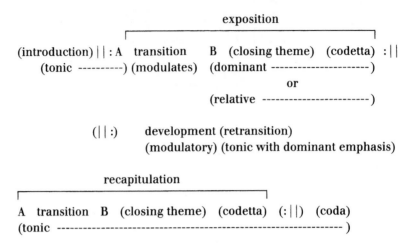

exposition

(introduction) || : A   transition   B   (closing theme)   (codetta)   : ||
          (tonic ----------) (modulates)   (dominant ---------------------)
                                                        or
                                              (relative -----------------------)

(|| :)   development (retransition)
          (modulatory) (tonic with dominant emphasis)

recapitulation

A   transition   B   (closing theme)   (codetta)   (: ||)   (coda)
(tonic --)

VIII. The distinguishing characteristic of *rondo form* is the alternation of an initial section, A, with contrasting sections. The A sections usually occur in the tonic key, and the alternating sections in contrasting keys. Rondos are typically in five or seven parts in the following designs:

A B A C A(A′)
A B A B′ A(A′)
A B A C A B′ A′
A B A C A D A(A′)

IX. *Sonata-rondo form* is a seven-part rondo in which the fourth part, C, is developmental. The key plan closely resembles that of sonata form:

A	B	A	C	A	B	A
(tonic)	(dominant or relative)	(tonic)	(developmental) (modulatory)	(tonic--------------------)		

21 Checklist for Analysis

All music should be analyzed as fully as possible within the limits of the student's knowledge at any stage of learning. Not only the individual elements but also their interaction should be studied. Following is a checklist of elements that should be included in an analysis.

I. Harmonic language.

   A. All keys and chords, with roman numerals and figured-bass symbols, or appropriate contemporary nomenclature. How are the key and mode established?

   B. All modulations, indicating type and placement.

   C. All cadences, indicating type and placement.

   D. All nonharmonic tones, by type.

   E. Functional and nonfunctional use of chromaticism.

   F. Use of nonfunctional (linear or coloristic) chords.

II. Large and small formal units.

   A. Phrases and periods, if any; phrase-groups; extensions and elisions.

   B. Overall form, including large letters for main sections and formal label, if appropriate. Note balance and proportion of sections.

   C. Use of repetition, altered repetition, departure, return, altered return, development, and contrast. Note the use of developmental devices.

   D. Elements of unity versus elements of variety.

   E. Stable versus unstable areas (tension versus relaxation).

III. Melodic organization.

   A. Motivic structure, both melodic and rhythmic.

   B. Melodic structure, including departure note and goal note, contour, climax, main structural pitches, range, and tessitura.

   C. Special aspects, such as contrapuntal devices and sequence.

IV. Rhythmic organization.

   A. Surface rhythm, meter, and harmonic rhythm.

   B. Special devices of rhythmic development.

   C. How the meter is emphasized or obscured.

   D. Tempo.

V. Sound.

   A. Use of the medium: idiomatic devices, range and tessitura, and timbre (color).

   B. Texture.

   C. Dynamics.

VI. Text-setting, where appropriate.

   A. Relations between form and/or mood of text and music.

   B. Rhythmic and/or metric relationships.

Sample Analysis

Observations

1. The form is simple binary: || : A: || : B: ||.
2. Each section is a parallel period consisting of two 4-measure phrases.
3. There is new motivic material and a new figuration in the B section.
4. Harmonic rhythm.

    a. A section: slow.

       for the first six measures.

       for the last two measures.

    b. B section: faster, slowing at cadence.

       (each phrase)

5. The background rhythm consists of eighth-note motion throughout, passing from the accompanimental figuration in the A section to the melodic material in the B section, and coming to rest in the final measure.

VII. The following aspects of any tonal contrapuntal work should be carefully observed and analyzed.

A. Individual lines.

1. Main motives (melodic and rhythmic).
2. Melodic intervals (types used and their placement in the phrase).
3. Cadence idioms.
4. Sequences (length, number of repetitions, and transposition).
5. Compound line, if any.
6. Climax placement.
7. Main structural pitches.

B. Relationships between lines.

1. Directional relationships (contrary, parallel, similar, or oblique).
2. Rhythmic relationships.
3. Motivic relationships (imitation, or bass line with predominant melody).
4. Intervallic relationships (on both strong and weak beats as well as at cadence points; analyze all the dissonances carefully).
5. Harmonic relationships (keys and harmonic implications, in roman numerals).

Sample Analysis

Gavotte I from English Suite no. 3   J. S. Bach

Observations

1. The form is the first half of a binary suite movement, modulating to the relative key by common chord (measure 6). Measures 1 through 8 form a parallel period.

2. Main motive.

3. Reduction to principal structural pitches (for an explanation of symbols, see Part V, Unit 18).

4. Other observations.

   a. The bass line is largely independent and nonimitative.
   b. Melodically, seconds and thirds predominate.
   c. There is a mixture of types of directional relationships, with no single type predominating.
   d. Rhythmically, the voices are about equally active, with the upper voice only slightly dominant.
   e. Imperfect consonances predominate between voices, except at cadence points, where there are tonic notes.
   f. Nonharmonic tones are mainly passing tones and neighbors.
   g. Notice the typical cadential figure in the bass in measures 7 and 8.
   h. The upper voice forms a compound line in measures 1, 2, 3, 5, and 7.

VIII. The following are additional questions for the analysis of twentieth-century music.

   A. Tonal centers, if any.

      1. How are they established?
      2. Do they change?

   B. Scalar materials.

      1. What type or types are employed?
      2. Do they change, or are they inflected?

   C. Harmonic vocabulary.

      1. What type of chord structures are used?
      2. Is chord succession systematic? If so, how?

   D. Special metric and rhythmic characteristics.

22 Composition Checklist

The following list should be used for reference when doing the free creative projects suggested in this book. Some of the following considerations may not apply in the early stages or in Part IV.

I. Form.

    A. Sections (tonal, cadential, or thematic) are clearly articulated.

    B. Phrases are clear and generally regular.

    C. The climax is clear and well placed.

    D. Contrast, repetition, and return are used where appropriate.

    E. All sections are proportionally balanced.

II. Harmony.

    A. Types of cadences are clear, well placed, and prepared.

    B. Functional progressions predominate.

    C. The harmonic rhythm generally is steady and regular.

    D. Altered chords are well placed in the phrase and not overused.

    E. Nonharmonic tone use is normal (motivic or sequential).

III. Line.

    A. There is a sense of contour (departure, curve, and arrival).

    B. There is a clear tonal organization.

    C. There is a linear and directional bass line.

    D. The outer-voice contrapuntal framework is effective.

    E. The motivic control (melodic and rhythmic) is tight.

    F. There is thematic clarity and consistency.

IV. Rhythm.

    A. There is metrical clarity and consistency.

    B. The rhythm is steady and regular, with a clear feeling of pattern.

    C. Rhythmic motion continues over weak cadence points.

V. Other matters.

    A. Accompaniment patterns are appropriate and consistent.

    B. There is overall textural consistency.

    C. There is thematic balance between players, where appropriate.

    D. Instrumental and vocal writing is idiomatic.

    E. The editing of score and parts is careful and complete.

    F. Notation is clear and complete.

    G. There is normal word and syllable stress in text-setting.

    H. Careful attention is paid to transpositions.

    I. There is appropriate use of dynamics and tempo gradations.

23 Instrumental Ranges and Transpositions

The registers indicated here are recommended for classroom use.

Woodwinds	Written Range	Actual Sound
flute		as written
oboe		as written
Bb clarinet		M2 lower
bass clarinet		M9 lower
bassoon		as written
Eb alto saxophone		M6 lower
Bb tenor saxophone		M9 lower
Eb baritone saxophone		M13 lower (P8 + M6 lower)

Brass	**Written Range**	**Actual Sound**
French horn in F		P5 lower
B♭ trumpet		M2 lower (C trumpet = as written)
trombone, euphonium		as written
tuba		as written

Strings	**Written Range**	**Actual Sound**
violin		as written
viola		as written
cello		as written
double bass		P8 lower

Bibliography

Important General Works

Bent, Ian, with William Drabkin. *Analysis*. New York: Norton, 1987.

Berry, Wallace. *Form in Music*. Englewood Cliffs, N.J.: Prentice-Hall, 2nd ed., 1986.

Dunsby, Jonathan, and Arnold Whittall. *Music Analysis in Theory and Practice*. New Haven: Yale University Press, 1988.

Goldman, Richard Franko. *Harmony in Western Music*. New York: Norton, 1965.

Green, Douglass. *Form in Tonal Music*, 2nd ed. New York: Holt, Rinehart and Winston, 1979.

Hepokoski, James and Warren Darcy. *Elements of Sonata Theory: Norms, Types, and Deformations in the Late-Eighteenth-Century Sonata*, New York: Oxford University Press, 2006.

Karkoschka, Erhard. *Notation in New Music: A Critical Guide to Interpretation and Realisation*. Translated by Ruth Koenig. New York: Praeger, 1972.

Kohs, Ellis B. *Musical Form: Studies in Analysis and Synthesis*. Boston: Houghton Mifflin, 1976.

LaRue, Jan. *Guidelines for Style Analysis*, expanded 2nd ed. Sterling Heights, MI: Harmonie Park Press, 2011.

Read, Gardner. *Music Notation: A Manual of Modern Practice*, 2nd ed. New York: Taplinger, 1979.

Salzer, Felix. *Structural Hearing*. New York: Dover, 1962.

Schenker, Heinrich. *Five Graphic Musical Analyses*. New York: Dover, 2012.

———. *Free Composition*. Translated and edited by Ernst Oster. New York: Longman, 1979.

———. *Harmony*. Edited by Jonas Oswald. Translated by Elizabeth Borgese. Chicago: University of Chicago Press, 1980.

Schoenberg, Arnold. *Structural Functions of Harmony*, rev. ed. Edited by Leonard Stein. New York: Norton, 1969.

Stone, Kurt. *Music Notation in the Twentieth Century*. New York: Norton, 1980.

Toch, Ernst. *Shaping Forces in Music*. New York: Dover, 1977.

Counterpoint

Benjamin, Thomas. *The Craft of Tonal Counterpoint*, 2nd ed. New York: Routledge, 2003.

Gauldin, Robert. *A Practical Approach to Eighteenth-Century Counterpoint*, rev. ed. Long Grove, Ill.: Waveland Press, 2013.

Kennan, Kent. *Counterpoint: Based on Eighteenth Century Practice*, 4th ed. Upper Saddle River, N.J.: Prentice-Hall, 1999.

Piston, Walter. *Counterpoint*. New York: Norton, 1947.

Rudiments Workbooks

Clendinning, Jane, Elizabeth West Marvin, and Joel Phillips. *The Musician's Guide to Fundamentals*, 2nd ed. New York: W.W. Norton, 2014.

Damschroder, David. *Foundations of Music and Musicianship*, 3rd ed. Belmont, Calif.: Schirmer, 2006.

Harder, Paul O., and Greg A. Steinke. *Basic Materials in Music Theory*, 12th ed. Englewood Cliffs, N.J.: Prentice-Hall, 2009.

Nelson, Robert, and Carl J. Christensen. *Foundations of Music: With Premium Website Access*, 8th ed. Boston, MA: Schirmer-Cengage Learning, 2014.

Twentieth-Century Techniques

Antokoletz, Elliott. *Twentieth Century Music*. Englewood Cliffs, N.J.: Prentice-Hall, 1991.

Brindle, Reginald Smith. *Serial Composition*. London: Oxford University Press, 1968.

Cope, David. *New Directions in Music*, 7th ed. Dubuque: William C. Brown, 2000.

———. *New Music Composition*, 4th ed. New York: Schirmer Books, 1985.

Dallin, Leon. *Techniques of Twentieth Century Composition*, 3rd ed. Dubuque: William C. Brown, 1974.

DeLone, Richard, et al., eds. *Aspects of Twentieth-Century Music*. Englewood Cliffs, N.J.: Prentice-Hall, 1974.

Forte, Allen. *The Structure of Atonal Music*. New Haven: Yale University Press, 1977.

Hanson, Howard. *Harmonic Materials of Modern Music*. New York: Appleton-Century-Crofts, 1960.

Hindemith, Paul. *The Craft of Musical Composition*. London: Schott Music, 1942 (Book I) and 1941 (Book II).

Kostka, Stefan. *Materials and Techniques of Post-Tonal Music*, 4th ed. Englewood Cliffs, N.J.: Prentice-Hall, 2011.

Lester, Joel. *Analytic Approaches to Twentieth Century Music*. New York: Norton, 1989.

Nyman, Michael. *Experimental Music*, 2nd ed. Cambridge: Cambridge University Press, 1999.

Perle, George. *Serial Composition and Atonality*, 6th ed. Berkeley: University of California Press, 1991.

Persichetti, Vincent. *Twentieth-Century Harmony: Creative Aspects and Practices*. New York: Norton, 1961.

Rahn, John. *Basic Atonal Theory*. New York: Longman, 1980.

Reti, Rudolph. *Tonality in Modern Music*. New York: Macmillan, 1962.

Straus, Joseph. *Introduction to Post-Tonal Theory*, 3rd ed. Englewood Cliffs, N.J.: Prentice-Hall, 2005.

Ulehia, Ludmilla. *Contemporary Harmony*. New York: Free Press, 1966.

Electronic Music

Dodge, Charles, and Thomas A. Jarse. *Computer Music*, 2nd ed. New York: Schirmer-Cengage Learning, 1997.

Hofstetter, Fred T. *Computer Literacy for Musicians*. Englewood Cliffs, N.J.: Prentice-Hall, 1988.

Holmes, Thomas B. *Electronic and Experimental Music: Technology, Music, and Culture*, 4th ed. London: Routledge, 2012.

Moore, Richard. *Elements of Computer Music*. Englewood Cliffs, N.J.: Prentice-Hall, 1990.

Schwartz, Elliott. *Electronic Music*. New York: Praeger, 1985.

Strange, Allen. *Electronic Music*, 2nd ed. Dubuque: William C. Brown, 1982.

Winsor, Phil. *Computer Assisted Music Composition*. Princeton, N.J.: Petrocelli Books, 1990.

Musical Anthologies

Benjamin, Thomas, Michael Horvit, and Robert Nelson. *Music for Analysis: Examples from the Common-Practice Period and the Twentieth Century*, 7th ed. New York: Oxford University Press, 2009.

Burkhart, Charles. *Anthology for Musical Analysis*, 7th ed. Boston, MA: Schirmer Cengage Learning, 2012.

Kotska, Stefan, and Roger Graybill. *Anthology of Music for Analysis*. Englewood Cliffs, N.J.: Prentice-Hall, 2003.

Melcher, Robert, Willard Warch, and Paul Mast. *Music for Study*, 3rd ed. Englewood Cliffs, N.J.: Prentice-Hall, 1988.

Wennerstrom, Mary. *Anthology of Twentieth Century Music*, 2nd ed. Englewood Cliffs, N.J.: Prentice-Hall, 1988.

Orchestration

Adler, Samuel. *The Study of Orchestration*, 3rd ed. New York: Norton, 2002.

Jacob, Gordon. *Elements of Orchestration*. New York: October House, 1965.

Kennan, Kent, and Donald Grantham. *The Technique of Orchestration*, 6th ed. Upper Saddle River, N.J.: Prentice-Hall, 2002.

Piston, Walter. *Orchestration*. New York: Norton, 1955.

Index